GUIDE FOR CELEBRATING INFANT BAPTISM

SECOND EDITION

TIMOTHY A. JOHNSTON
PAUL TURNER
PAUL RADKOWSKI

LITURGY TRAINING PUBLICATIONS

Nihil Obstat
Rev. Mr. Daniel G. Welter, JD
Chancellor
Archdiocese of Chicago
October 4, 2019

Imprimatur
Most Rev. Ronald A. Hicks
Vicar General
Archdiocese of Chicago
October 4, 2019

The *Nihil Obstat* and *Imprimatur* are declarations that the material is free from doctrinal or moral error, and thus is granted permission to publish in accordance with c. 827. No legal responsibility is assumed by the grant of this permission. No implication is contained herein that those who have granted the *Nihil Obstat* and *Imprimatur* agree with the content, opinions, or statements expressed.

GUIDE FOR CELEBRATING INFANT BAPTISM, SECOND EDITION © 2020 Archdiocese of Chicago: Liturgy Training Publications, 3949 South Racine Avenue, Chicago, IL 60609; 800-933-1800; fax: 800-933-7094; email: orders@ltp.org; website: www.LTP.org. All rights reserved.

This book is part of the *Preparing Parish Worship*™ series.

This book was edited by Danielle A. Noe. Víctor R. Pérez was the production editor, Anna Manhart was the designer, and Kari Nicholls was the production artist. Updates pertaining to the English translation of the *Order of Baptism of Children* were made by Danielle A. Noe.

Art on page viii © Martin Erspamer, OSB; photos on pages 12, 18, 44, 76, and 86 © John Zich; photo on page 14 © Dennis Jarvis courtesy Wikimedia Commons; cover photo and interior photos on pages 30, 46, 51, 58, 61, 64, 70, 122, 125, 126, and 128 © Liturgy Training Publications.

24 23 22 21 20   1 2 3 4 5

Printed in the United States of America

Library of Congress Control Number: 2019953414

ISBN 978-1-61671-564-9

EGCIB2

Timothy and Paul R.
dedicate this book with gratitude
to Fr. Allan R. Bouley, OSB,
whose teaching has inspired them to
prepare the rites well and celebrate them joyfully.

CONTENTS

PREFACE vii

WELCOME x

The Theological and Historical
  Developments of Infant Baptism   1
Preparing the Order of Baptism of Children   20
  Parish Preparation Team   23
  Pastoral Issues   29
  Order of Baptism of Children within Mass   35
  Order of Baptism for Several Children   79
  Order of Baptism for One Child   87
  Order of Baptism for a Large
    Number of Children   90
  Order of Baptism of Children
    to Be Used by Catechists in
    the Absense of a Priest or Deacon   95
  Order of Baptism of Children in Danger
    of Death, or at the Point of Death, to Be
    Used in the Absence of a Priest or Deacon   102
  Order of Bringing a Baptized Child to the Church   109
  Other Important Pastoral Considerations   114

Frequently Asked Questions   129

RESOURCES   151

GLOSSARY   157

ACKNOWLEDGMENTS   164

PREFACE

"Twins!" Crispus shouted. "A boy and a girl!" He raced past his joyous servants out the front door of his house and into the street to announce the news to his neighbors. "Twins!" He raced back in through the same doors and past the same servants to see his lovely wife Rebekah, her face flushed, smiling broadly.

She gushed, "I thought that this child was simply going to be larger than Samuel was. I didn't realize . . ."

"Twins!" Crispus exclaimed to his wife, who obviously knew this already.

"Yes, dear," she laughed, holding a newborn in each arm.

Neighbors ran over to celebrate. Some dashed out of the synagogue. They were accustomed to seeing Crispus on more somber occasions—guiding them with sincere devotion through their Sabbath prayers.[1] They had never seen him so full of life. They loved his excitement about his rapidly growing family.

"No. You can't come in," insisted Leah, the maidservant, when Hulda tried to enter. "Give Rebekah some privacy. You will see the twins in due time." Leah and the other servants protected their patrons as if they were part of the family too.

As Crispus received the happy crowd at his door, a blur across the street drew his attention. The door in the house next to the synagogue had opened. Someone was exiting.[2] Crispus looked up, over the assembled throng on his doorstep, expecting to see his somewhat faithful friend Titus Justus walk out.[3] But instead, a short, bald man made a quick, furtive exit and started walking up the road. The man noticed the crowd across the way, turned his head, and caught the eyes of Crispus. Then he looked down, quickened his pace, and proceeded up the street and away.

"Paul!" Crispus called out. The man stopped. Crispus pushed through the crowd to meet up with the man on the street.

---

1. See Acts of the Apostles 18:8.
2. See Acts of the Apostles 18:7.
3. See Acts of the Apostles 18:7.

Paul looked surprised. "I thought you wouldn't want to see me."

"What? No. That's crazy," said Crispus, reaching out to shake Paul's hand.

"What's all the excitement?" Paul asked.

"Twins!" said Crispus. "My wife just gave birth to a boy and a girl. We are surprised and happy as can be. My son Samuel will be a wonderful big brother."

"Congratulations, Crispus," said Paul. "I didn't mean to ignore you. I just thought that you wouldn't want to see me because, as you well know, things have not gone well between the synagogue and me."

"Paul, I am a synagogue official.[4] I recognize faith when I see it. I've heard you. Your belief that Jesus is the Messiah is compelling. I was disappointed when I saw what happened last week when some of my own friends opposed you and reviled you."[5]

"Can you blame them? I said some strong words."

"I still remember those words: 'Your blood be on your heads! I am clear of responsibility. From now on I will go to the Gentiles.'"[6]

Paul winced as he heard Crispus repeat verbatim what he had said. "I wasn't talking about you," Paul admitted. "You have always been kind. Even Titus Justus says so."

Exhilarated over the birth of his children and humbled by the presence of the great Apostle Paul, Crispus moved the conversation further. "I have not admitted this to anyone, Paul, not even to Rebekah." He leaned closer and whispered. "I believe you."

Paul looked up sharply. He squeezed his friend's arm. Crispus begged him, "I want to learn more."

By now the crowd at the door of Crispus' house was getting restless. "Isn't that Paul?" Hulda asked, fixing her gaze into the street. "Why is Crispus talking to him? Has he forgotten his own newborn children?"

---

4. See Acts of the Apostles 18:8.
5. See Acts of the Apostles 18:6.
6. Acts of the Apostles 18:6.

Paul feared that another crowd was growing restless. "Go to your house," he said to Crispus. "All right," he answered. "But I want my household to go to you."

Some time later, Crispus, along with his entire household and many of the Corinthians who heard Paul, believed and were baptized.[7]

Faith in Jesus Christ resounds so strongly in the hearts of believers that they want to share it with others, especially with those whom they love, even their children.

—Paul Turner

---

7. See Acts of the Apostles 18:8.

WELCOME

Welcome to *Guide for Celebrating Infant Baptism, Second Edition*. Before his Ascension into heaven, Jesus commanded the disciples to "Go . . . and make disciples of all nations, baptizing them in the name of the Father, and of the Son, and of the holy Spirit."[1] Just as the early Church was commanded to go forth, the Church today continues to announce the Good News of Jesus Christ. The celebration of Baptism is a sign of the Church's missionary activity of showing the world God's love and mercy. When the Church, Christ's Body, gathers to welcome someone into God's family, it is a gift and proclamation of God's goodness and saving action. Baptism is "the door to life and to the kingdom";[2] it is the sacrament that has "incorporated us into Christ . . . and formed [us] us into the People of God."[3] This alone stirs joy within the community, especially those who prepare families for the celebration and those who prepare the liturgy, so that Baptism is celebrated reverently, fully, and intentionally for the whole community. The celebration of Baptism reminds us that God has called each of us to be missionary disciples who announce his Kingdom. Celebrating Baptism well has the potential to evangelize and transform a parish community so that faith will be stirred and deepened.

About This Book

This book is designed to support priests, deacons, liturgists, musicians, directors of religious formation and education, and catechists who are directly involved with the preparation and celebration of the Sacrament of Baptism. This resource will help ministers more easily explore and understand the possibilities found in the rubrics of the recently retranslated *Order of Baptism of Children*. The ministry of preparation is a great gift to the parish community,

---

1. Matthew 28:19.
2. *Christian Initiation*, General Introduction (CI), 3.
3. CI, 2.

but not always an easy task. This book will help you facilitate the preparation process with other staff members, parents, and family members.

The book includes three sections. The first section of the book surveys both the history of Baptism within the Catholic tradition and its sacramental theology. Having a solid foundation in these two areas provides us with insight into our current practice and understanding of the sacrament. Before preparing a Baptism, it is important that we begin here.

The second section is a practical one as it walks the reader through the options found in the official ritual texts. It provides an overview of the ritual book as well as the other liturgical books needed for the liturgy; discusses the parish preparation team and its roles and gives suggestions to assist the team with preparing the sacramental liturgy; and addresses the particular circumstances of Baptism: when it can be celebrated in relation to the liturgical calendar or other contexts, what is necessary for Baptism, and who is the proper minister of the sacrament. This practical section will also assist those who are responsible for choosing music for the liturgy and those who oversee designing the liturgical environment as well as guiding parish preparation teams through the various rituals and their nuances: (1) Baptism celebrated within Mass, (2) Baptism celebrated without Mass, (3) Baptism celebrated by a catechist, (4) Baptism in danger of death, and (5) bringing a baptized child to the Church.

The final sections consist of frequently asked questions to help guide the team and families when preparing the liturgy as well as an annotated list of resources on Baptism and liturgy and a glossary for quick reference.

The Church's baptismal liturgy is filled with rich symbols that invite us to contemplate the Paschal Mystery. May this guide deepen your understanding and appreciation of the *Order of Baptism of Children* as you work to glorify God in your ministry.

About the Authors

TIMOTHY A. JOHNSTON is an editor and liturgical training consultant for Liturgy Training Publications in Chicago, Illinois. He also serves as the director of liturgy at Immaculate Conception parish in Chicago's Brighton Park neighborhood. He earned a master of arts in liturgical studies from St. John's University, Minnesota, and a master of arts in Christian doctrine from Marquette University, Wisconsin. His bachelor of science in music education was granted by Quincy University, Illinois. Originally from Old Mines, Missouri, Timothy previously served as the director of the Office of Liturgy for the Diocese of Salt Lake City, the director of the Office of Worship for the Diocese of St. Cloud, and as director of Liturgical Programs at Marquette University. He has served as a high school teacher, written articles, and presented workshops on liturgical formation.

Paul Turner is pastor of the Cathedral of the Immaculate Conception in Kansas City, Missouri, and director of the Office of Divine Worship for the Diocese of Kansas City-St. Joseph. He holds a doctorate in sacred theology from Sant'Anselmo in Rome. His publications include *At the Supper of the Lamb* (Chicago: Liturgy Training Publications, 2011); *Glory in the Cross* (Collegeville: Liturgical Press, 2011); and *Celebrating Initiation: A Guide for Priests* (Chicago: World Library Publications, 2008). He is a former President of the North American Academy of Liturgy, a member of Societas Liturgica and the Catholic Academy of Liturgy. He is a recipient of the Jubilate Deo Award (National Association of Pastoral Musicians) and the Frederick McManus Award (Federation of Diocesan Liturgical Commissions). He serves as a facilitator for the International Commission on English in the Liturgy.

Paul Radkowski is the director of music at the Church of St. Edward the Confessor in Granville, Ohio, where he also serves as a campus minister at Denison University. He earned a master of arts in liturgical studies from St. John's University, Collegeville, Minnesota, and a bachelor of arts in English from the University of Notre Dame. Originally from West Middlesex, Pennsylvania, he was previously the liturgy and music coordinator at the Church of St. Peter in St. Cloud, Minnesota. In addition to writing articles and giving presentations on liturgical and theological topics, he has served as a high school teacher and as a musician at numerous parishes. He lives in Ohio with his wife and children.

The Theological and Historical Developments of Infant Baptism

"Through the Sacraments of Christian Initiation all who have been freed from the power of darkness and have died, been buried and been raised wtih Christ, receive the Spirit of filial adoption and celebrate with the entire People of God the memorial of the Lord's Death and Resurrection."

—*Christian Initiation*, General Introduction, 1

Just as good parents provide for the needs of children born into their family, so does the Church. Throughout Christian history the Catholic Church has offered children the sacraments of initiation. The practice has changed according to the sensibilities of different times and cultures, but the Church has consistently expressed a parental solicitude for children.

All the sacraments participate in divine grace. In fact, God acts first. God's grace offers salvation to all.[1] Through the sacraments, the Church welcomes children to participate in the divine life of Christ. The Baptism of infant children is a response to God's gracious invitation. Infant Baptism relies on no prior demonstration of the child's worthiness. It is the Church's response to God's gift of life and invitation to grace. The Catholic Church believes that Baptism is "the door to life and to the kingdom."[2]

> For the grace of God has appeared, saving all and training us to reject godless ways and worldly desires and to live temperately, justly, and devoutly in this age, as we await the blessed hope, the appearance of the glory of the great God and of our savior Jesus Christ.
>
> —Titus 2:11–13

Evidence suggests that infants were baptized from the beginning of Christian history. This early testimony is not totally conclusive, and therefore some people have doubted that baptizing infants fell among the intentions of the Apostles and leaders of the early Church. Nonetheless, parents in those days lived in an exciting

---

1. See Titus 2:11.
2. CI, 3.

environment of evangelization in which the Baptism of infants logically could have flourished.

Baptism in Scripture

The New Testament offers no conclusive evidence for the Baptism of children. However, there is circumstantial evidence for it. Acts of the Apostles includes several reports of Baptisms, some in great numbers, others in small groups, and even some of individuals. The book offers a discernible pattern of household Baptisms in the years following the Resurrection.

- Crispus, a synagogue official, and his household, after hearing the preaching of St. Paul, became believers and were baptized.[3]
- Lydia and her household did the same.[4]
- Paul and Silas walked out of prison after an earthquake unfettered their chains. The jailer responsible for their care came to faith in Christ after observing their miraculous release. He and his entire household were baptized.[5]
- Peter was preaching to the household of Cornelius when the gathered assembly started manifesting gifts of the Holy Spirit. Peter ordered the Baptism of them all.[6]

> Believe in the Lord Jesus and you and your household will be saved.
> —Acts of the Apostles 16:31

Outside of Acts similar evidence persists. St. Paul admits to performing Baptisms on only one occasion—for the household of Stephanas.[7] In John's account of the Gospel, after Jesus had cured the son of a royal official, that man and all his household believed in Jesus.[8] Although this event predates testimony of Christian Baptism, all of which followed the Resurrection, the story fits a pattern in which belief spread from one individual's experience throughout an entire household.

None of these reports explicitly says that infants were among the members of the household. But it is hard to imagine that they were not; harder

---

3. See Acts of the Apostles 18:8.
4. See Acts of the Apostles 16:11–15.
5. See Acts of the Apostles 16:29–33.
6. See Acts of the Apostles 10:44–48.
7. See 1 Corinthians 1:16.
8. See John 4:46b, 53b.

still to imagine parents agreeing that small children in their house were too young to be baptized. Even in the stories about large group Baptisms, such as three thousand persons on the day of Pentecost,[9] it is unlikely that the Apostles solicitously excluded the youngest among them, especially since Peter had just explicitly promised the gift of the Holy Spirit to his listeners and to their children.[10]

Within his treatment of Christian family life, Paul took up the problem of believers marrying unbelievers. He said that the believer made the unbelieving spouse holy, and their children were holy.[11] The holiness of the children does not conclusively argue that they were baptized, but the pastoral concern for the spiritual life of children is evident, an atmosphere in which their Baptism could easily have been tolerated, if not encouraged.

Furthermore, Paul compared Baptism to the Jewish ceremony of circumcision.[12] Although he was making the broader point that adult Gentile converts need not be circumcised, Paul thought of Baptism as a ceremony that shares some significance with a Jewish rite normally performed on infants.

> Let the children come to me and do not prevent them; for the kingdom of God belongs to such as these.
>
> —Luke 18:16

In general, Jesus showed interest in children as he did for others marginalized in society. He forbade people to keep children from him and said that one enters the Kingdom of God like a child.[13] He said that those who welcomed a child welcomed him.[14]

In summary, the New Testament describes an environment in which children were welcomed and households were baptized. It seems logical that the first Christians baptized children.

Early Church History

Clear evidence for the Baptism of infants finally surfaced by the end of the second century. One reason for the appearance of this evidence is the

---

9. See Acts of the Apostles 2:41.
10. See Acts of the Apostles 2:39.
11. See 1 Corinthians 7:14.
12. See Colossians 2:11–12.
13. See Mark 10:14–15; Matthew 19:14–15; Luke 18:16–17.
14. See Luke 9:48; Matthew 18:3–5.

controversy surrounding the practice. Origen of Alexandria (†253) favored the Baptism of infants.[15] Tertullian of Carthage (†220) opposed it.[16] Objections subsided rather quickly. Cyprian of Carthage (†258) supported baptizing infants immediately after their birth.[17] *The Apostolic Tradition* (third through fourth centuries) describes an elaborate initiation ceremony in which catechumens were baptized, anointed, and given Communion. During the liturgy, the first among them to participate in all these ceremonies were infants too young to speak or walk.[18]

Already in the fourth and fifth centuries, the rationale for baptizing children migrated to a concern about Original Sin. Because so many adults had already been baptized, the percentage of infants being baptized rose. The Church understood that Baptism cleansed adults of the sins that they had committed. Infants, however, had not committed personal sin, yet they were still being baptized. The explanation focused more and more on a cleansing from Original Sin, a sin into which every human being is born. If left unchecked, Original Sin exposes a person to moral dangers. Christ is the remedy for this sin. As St. Paul wrote, "For just as through the disobedience of one person the many were made sinners, so through the obedience of one the many will be made righteous."[19] Furthermore, the high infant mortality rate caused many infants to die before Baptism. Through the teaching on Original Sin the Church promoted the Baptism of infants, all of whom were, in a literal sense, in danger of death.

Among the Church fathers, St. Ambrose of Milan (†397) first treated this theme. He argued from the Jewish practice of circumcision, which was introduced for infants because "sin exists from infancy. . . . The infant must be called back from sin," wrote Ambrose. He recalled Jesus' words in John's account of the Gospel: "Unless you have been born again by water and the Holy Spirit, you cannot enter into the reign of God."[20] Ambrose held that this teaching of Christ excludes no one, not even an infant.

St. Augustine (†430) drew an even stronger and more fearsome conclusion: "Unbaptized children cannot have life, and for this reason are sentenced

---

15. See Paul Turner, *Ages of Initiation: The First Two Christian Millennia* (Collegeville, MN: Liturgical Press, 2000): [CD] chapter 2, part 7.
16. See Turner, chapter 2, part 7.
17. See Turner, chapter 2, part 7.
18. See Turner, chapter 2, part 7.
19. Romans 5:19.
20. Turner, chapter 3, part 7; see also John 3:5.

nonetheless with eternal death, though more tolerably than all who commit their own sins."[21] Augustine painted a bleak picture for families mourning the death of a newborn. Indeed, citing the end of Mark's account of the Gospel, "whoever does not believe will be condemned,"[22] Augustine wrote, "If by the words of the gospel you are driven to confess that children who are dying cannot have life and salvation unless they have been baptized, ask yourselves, 'Why must those who are not baptized be compelled to undergo the judgment of the second death, when he who condemns no one unworthily will be judging?' and you will find what you don't want to find: original sin."[23]

The Council of Carthage (418) inserted the teaching on Original Sin into its canons: "Even children who have not yet been able themselves to commit any sin are therefore truly baptized for the forgiveness of sins, so that what they contracted by birth may be cleansed in them by rebirth."[24]

By the fifth century, when a typical bishop baptized new Christians, he continued the same ceremony with the Confirmation and First Communion of those he had just baptized regardless of their age—adults and infants alike. Priests and deacons baptized and gave Communion to the same unrestricted age group. Confirmation, however, was reserved to a bishop. A separate ceremony developed for bishops to confirm those who had been baptized by other ministers. A person's age did not matter; adults and infants were eligible for Baptism, Confirmation, and First Communion. The only reason Confirmation was deferred was one's limited access to a bishop, who had the authority to administer it.[25]

This same initiation practice persisted when the Church began to develop sacramentaries and orders of worship. For example, the *Gallican Order XV* (775–780) explained that a priest who baptized also gave Communion to all present—including the infants he had just baptized. Confirmation would wait until a bishop became available.[26]

When bishops baptized infants in the Middle Ages, they continued to offer full initiation, giving infants Confirmation and First Communion. For example, the *Roman Pontifical* of the twelfth century clearly instructs the

---

21. Turner, chapter 3, part 7.
22. Mark 16:16.
23. Turner, chapter 3, part 7.
24. Turner, chapter 3, part 7.
25. See Turner, chapter 4.
26. See Turner, chapter 5, part 7.

bishop to baptize, confirm, and give Communion to infants.[27] Because of the successful evangelization of Western Europe, the number of adults entering the catechumenate had dwindled, and the number of infant Baptisms had sharply risen. Nonetheless, ceremonial books continued to describe the full initiation rites when a bishop presided. Books were expensive to produce. Bishops were likely to command a market for them. Although these publications on adult Baptism repeated instructions copied from earlier centuries, twelfth-century candidates for initiation were almost exclusively infants.

A canon in the Fourth Lateran Council (1215) called for all to confess their sins at least once a year, beginning at the years of discretion.[28] This contributed to the pastoral practice of deferring First Communion from the baptismal ceremony to a later age. Because bishops were confirming so few infants at Baptism, the celebration of Confirmation was generally deferred from Baptism as well. Consequently, the gradual breakup of the unified initiation ceremony became more extensive by the thirteenth century. However, for well over the first one thousand Christian years the practice of giving Communion to infants endured in the Church, and bishops gave each child all three initiation sacraments in the same liturgy, whenever they baptized.

Only after the Protestant Reformation in the early sixteenth century did the Church establish a more universal minimum age for Confirmation.[29] Regional Church councils had done the same for several centuries, but the practice was not uniform or extensive. The Reformation uncovered a catechetical crisis in the Catholic Church. The publication of the *Catechism of the Council of Trent* addressed this need. Its appearance in 1566 actually preceded the beginning of Trent's liturgical reform by four years, which shows that the bishops perceived that the need for better catechesis outweighed the need for better liturgy. Although catechetical preparation for Confirmation was fairly minimal, it did provide some opportunity to educate the faithful on the basics of their faith. Some received Confirmation before their First Communion; others did not. The sequence of these sacraments had more to do with the availability of the bishop than with any catechetical plan.

These catechetical strategies became important because the practice of baptizing infants persisted. As Christian infants grew in age, the Church

---

27. See Turner, chapter 7, part 1.
28. See Turner, chapter 8, part 5.
29. *See* Turner, chapter 9, part 6.

offered them opportunities to grow in wisdom through formation linked to the reception of the sacraments.

The Post-Reformation Church

After the Council of Trent, the Catholic Church revised her ceremonies, combining them all into a single ritual book. The 1614 *Roman Ritual* opened with two versions of the baptismal ceremony, one for infants and one for adults. The adult ceremony gathered evidence for the various stages of the catechumenate as practiced in the early Church and compiled a single ritual for administering all of them together. The rite for infants simplified the proceedings, though the baptismal ritual remained complex.

The post-Tridentine *Roman Ritual*'s Order of the Baptism of Children remained in force from 1614 until 1969.[30] A priest or a deacon could lead the ceremony. For simplicity, the ritual—and the description of it that follows below—indicates how a priest baptizes. The same description applies to a deacon, with the sole exception that, in the moment when the ritual calls for it, he uses salt previously blessed by a priest. The ritual presents adaptations for circumstances when the priest baptizes more than one child at a time.

The priest opened the ceremony outside the nave of the church wearing a violet stole over his surplice.[31] He addressed two questions to the child, and the godparent made the response. The priest called the child by name and asked, "What are you seeking from the Church of God?" The godparent answered, "Faith." The priest asked the child, "What does faith offer you?" The godparent answered, "Eternal life." The priest continued with a catechetical instruction addressed to the uncomprehending infant: "If therefore you wish to enter into life, keep the commandments: You shall love the Lord your God with all your heart, with all your soul, and with all your mind, and your neighbor as yourself."[32]

The priest then blew air onto the child's face three times, and addressed Satan: "Go forth from him (her), unclean spirit, and give way to the Holy Spirit, the Paraclete." With his thumb, the priest traced the Sign of the Cross on the forehead and breast of the child, saying to the infant, "Receive the sign

---

30. See *The Roman Ritual in Latin and English with Rubrics and Plainchant Notation: The Sacraments and Processions*, trans. and ed. Philip T. Weller, vol. 1 (Boonville, NY: Preserving Christian Publications, 2007). Hereafter *Roman Ritual*. All translations of excerpts of this work from Latin into English are by the author.

31. See *Roman Ritual*, "De Sacramento Baptismi rite administrando," 37, p. 36.

32. *Roman Ritual*, 1–2, p. 36.

of the cross both on your forehead and on your heart. Put your trust in heavenly precepts. Act in such a way that you may be now the temple of God."[33] The priest offered a prayer to God for the child about to be baptized.

The priest placed his hand on the child's head and then stretched out the same hand, saying another prayer to God, this one asking God to drive Satan away. He next addressed the salt that would be used for the baptismal water, declaring that he was exorcising it to make it a sign of salvation. He put a bit of salt into the mouth of the infant and addressed the child by name, saying, "Receive the salt of wisdom; may it profit you for eternal life." Then the priest said to the infant, "Peace be with you," and someone—probably a server or the godparent although the person is not identified—answered, "And with your spirit."[34]

> If therefore you wish to enter into life, keep the commandments: You shall love the Lord your God with all your heart, with all your soul, and with all your mind, and your neighbor as yourself.
> —Roman Ritual, 3–4

The priest asked God to let the child be enriched with heavenly food. And he told the unclean spirit to flee the child in the name of the Trinity. He made the Sign of the Cross on the child's forehead and addressed the cursed devil never to return. He placed his hand on the child's head and then extended his hand for another prayer to God that the child might receive true knowledge. He placed the left end of his stole on the child and, calling the infant by name, brought the child into the church by saying, "Enter into the temple of God that you may share eternal life with Christ."[35]

Outside the font, the priest and the godparents prayed together the Apostles' Creed and the Lord's Prayer. The priest addressed "every unclean spirit," asking them to leave the infant. He took saliva from his mouth in order to touch the ears and nose of the infant, though this could be omitted for sanitary concerns. Touching the child's ears, the priest said, "Ephphetha, that is, Be opened." Touching the nose, he said, "To a sweet aroma. You, though, devil, flee, for the judgment of God is drawing near."[36]

The priest called the child by name and asked three questions: "Do you renounce Satan?" "And all his works?" "And all his pomps?" The godparent

---

33. *Roman Ritual*, 3–4, pp. 36–38.
34. *Roman Ritual*, 5–7, pp. 38–42.
35. *Roman Ritual*, 7–10, pp. 42–46.
36. *Roman Ritual*, 11–13, pp. 46–48.

responded "I renounce" on behalf of the child. Dipping his thumb in the oil of catechumens, the priest anointed the child on the breast and on the sternum ("between the shoulders") in the form of a cross, saying, "I anoint you with the oil of salvation in Christ Jesus our Lord, that you may have eternal life." The response, "Amen," was probably said by the godparent. With a cotton ball he then wiped away the extra oil from his thumb and off the child.[37]

The priest removed his violet stole and replaced it with a white one. He, the godparent, and the infant then all entered the baptistry. He called the child by name and asked, "Do you believe in God the Father almighty, creator of heaven and earth?" "Do you believe in Jesus Christ, his only Son our Lord, who was born and suffered?" "Do you believe in the Holy Spirit, the holy catholic Church, the communion of Saints, the forgiveness of sins, the resurrection of the body, and eternal life?" To all these questions the godparent responded on behalf of the child, "I believe." Once more calling the child by name, the priest asked, "Do you wish to be baptized?" The godparent on behalf of the child answered, "I do."[38]

The godparent—or both godparents—held the child while the priest, taking a small vessel or pitcher, poured baptismal water three times over the infant's head in the form of a cross, while carefully pronouncing the words of Baptism, calling the child by name: "I baptize you in the name of the Father, and of the Son, and of the Holy Spirit," pouring water at each of the three divine names. He was permitted to immerse the child, in which case he took the child carefully in his own hands and dipped the infant three times. The printed formula carries three red crosses; either these were simply copied over from the formula for pouring water in the Sign of the Cross, or they indicate the intention that even the immersion would take place by moving the entire child in the form of the cross in the water. The godparent or both godparents then lifted the child from the font, receiving the infant from the priest's hands.[39]

In those cases where a doubt persisted about the child's baptismal status, the priest called the child by name and said, "If you have not been baptized, I baptize you in the name of the Father, and of the Son, and of the Holy Spirit."[40]

---

37. See *Roman Ritual*, 14–16, pp. 48–50.
38. *Roman Ritual*, 17–18, p. 50.
39. See *Roman Ritual*, 19–21, pp. 50–52.
40. *Roman Ritual*, 22, p. 52.

Having placed his thumb into the vessel of sacred chrism, the priest anointed the crown of the infant's head with the Sign of the Cross while declaring that God the Father "anoints you with the chrism of salvation in the same Jesus Christ our Lord for eternal life." The godparents, presumably, are those who answered "Amen." The priest says, "Peace be with you," and the reply was made: "And with your spirit." With another cotton ball the priest wiped off the excess chrism from his thumb and from the child's head.[41]

The priest placed a while linen cloth on the child's head, saying, "Receive the white garment that you should carry clean before the throne of our Lord Jesus Christ, that you may have eternal life." Others answer, "Amen." The priest gave a lighted candle to the child or the godparent, saying, "Receive this burning candle and keep your Baptism irreproachable: Keep the commandments of God, so that, when the Lord comes at the wedding banquet, you may meet him together with all the saints in heaven, and may you live for ever and ever." Others answer, "Amen."[42]

> But you are "a chosen race, a royal priesthood, a holy nation, a people of his own, so that you may announce the praises" of him who called you out of darkness into his wonderful light.
> —1 Peter 2:9

Finally, the priest calls the child by name and says, "Go in peace, and may the Lord be with you." Others answer, "Amen."[43]

After the Second Vatican Council issued its groundbreaking *Constitution on the Sacred Liturgy*, this entire ritual was revised. The *Constitution* insisted that the revisions demonstrate that the infants are indeed infants.[44] It also asked that the duties of parents and godparents be made clearer. The revised ceremony reflects all these considerations. The priest now addresses fewer words to the infant, and instead talks more to the parents and godparents, invoking their responses and assigning them responsibilities. The number of exorcisms was diminished. The prayer accompanying the anointing with chrism was enhanced with a reference to one of the Council's most beloved biblical passages, 1 Peter 2:9. The child is anointed as a member of Christ, who is Priest, Prophet, and King.

---

41. See *Roman Ritual*, 23–24, p. 52.
42. *Roman Ritual*, 24–25, pp. 52–54.
43. *Roman Ritual*, 26, p. 54.
44. See *Constitution on the Sacred Liturgy* (CSL), 67: "The rite for the baptism of infants is to be revised and it should be suited to the fact that those to be baptized are infants. The roles as well as the obligations of parents and godparents should be brought out more clearly in the rite itself."

The *ephphatha* was moved after Baptism, and the words were changed to reflect the child's future role in the ministry of evangelization.

Theology of Baptism

Christian Initiation, General Introduction

The meaning of Christian initiation in the Catholic Church is neatly summarized in the first paragraphs of *Christian Initiation,* General Introduction, which opens both the *Order of Baptism of Children* (OBC) and the *Rite of Christian Initiation of Adults* (RCIA).

At the time of the Second Vatican Council, when scholars reviewed the rituals then in force, they considered both the adult and the infant baptismal ceremonies together. When they finished their work, they composed one general introduction for initiation and attached both revised ceremonies to it in a single volume. In the end, however, the Vatican published the rites of Baptism for children and for adult initiation separately, each beginning with the same general introduction.

The first paragraph of *Christian Initiation,* General Introduction, details the three main purposes of Christian initiation, without ever mentioning the sacraments by name. These sacraments free us "from the power of darkness"[45] and we are "buried and . . . raised with Christ."[46] They bestow "the Spirit of filial adoption," and, through these sacraments, we celebrate "the memorial of the Lord's Death and Resurrection . . . with the entire People of God."[47] Even without the subsequent paragraphs, these sentences clearly refer to Baptism, Confirmation, and Eucharist. However, by omitting the names of the individual sacraments, the opening paragraph of *Christian Initiation* subtly proclaims that the initiation sacraments function as a unit. Even though each accomplishes something special, they all work together to achieve something grand.

> For, having been incorporated into Christ through Baptism, they are formed into the People of God, and, having received the remission of all their sins and been rescued from the power of darkness, they are brought to the status of adopted sons and daughters, being made a new creation by water and the Holy Spirit.
>
> —*Christian Initiation,* General Introduction, 2

---

45. CI, 2.
46. CI, 1.
47. CI, 1.

The second paragraph subdivides into sections that treat each initiation sacrament individually. The document asserts that Baptism incorporates us into Christ and forms us "into the People of God."[48] This statement voices a positive view toward the purpose of Baptism.

Prior to the Council, Catholics commonly learned a negative view: Baptism cleansed a person from Original Sin. It removed an obstacle to grace. The Church had embraced that definition largely because it supported the widespread pastoral practice of baptizing infants. The Church believes that Baptism cleanses a person from sin. The sins of an adult are easy to observe, but an infant is incapable of personal sin. Nonetheless, the Church believes that every human being is born with Original Sin,[49] which the *Catechism* calls a sin "contracted" not "committed."[50] Original Sin characterizes the human condition that needs salvation. Baptism cleanses a human from this contracted sin, which explains one of the purposes of infant Baptism.

"Baptism incorporates us into Christ and forms us into God's people" (*Christian Initiation*, General Introduction, 2).

Although it is still correct to say that Baptism cleanses a person from Original Sin, the second paragraph of *Christian Initiation, General Introduction*, stresses two other points: incorporation into the Body of Christ, and membership in God's people. Both concepts have strong biblical foundations. The letters of St. Paul call the community of the faithful the Body of Christ.[51] The First Letter of Peter calls the same community God's own people.[52] The doctrine of Original Sin indicates what Baptism leaves behind, whereas the ideas of the Body of Christ and the people of God show where Baptism leads.

Christian Initiation, General Introduction, makes other points about Baptism. It reaffirms that Baptism pardons all sins and rescues people "from the power of darkness."[53] This relates to the foregoing point about Original

---

48. CI, 2.
49. Mary, because she was to become the mother of Jesus, is the lone exception. She was conceived without Original Sin, and therefore holds the title of the Immaculate Conception.
50. *Catechism of the Catholic Church* (CCC), 404.
51. See 1 Corinthians 12:27 and Romans 12:5.
52. See 1 Peter 2:9–10.
53. CI, 2.

Sin, but the introduction places these purposes of Baptism into a secondary field. It addresses the combat with sin and Satan only after proclaiming the victory of Jesus Christ.

To conclude its initial reflection on Baptism, *Christian Initiation,* General Introduction, presents a mystical concept: the baptized are "a new creation," "sons and daughters" and "children of God."[54] The Church unflinchingly teaches that Jesus Christ is the only-begotten Son of God. The New Testament affirms that those who follow him are also children of God,[55] and Jesus himself taught his followers to call upon God in prayer as their "Father." To distinguish Christ from Christians, the Church's tradition stresses that Jesus is the only-begotten Son of God, but every Christian is an adopted child of God. St. Paul explores this analogy in two of his letters.[56] Baptism bestows an incomparable inheritance upon God's children.

> [We] are called, and indeed are, children of God.
>
> *Christian Initiation,* General Introduction, 2

The Church's message on the purpose of Baptism brims with analogies: "Baptism is the Sacrament by which human beings are incorporated into the Church and are built up together into a dwelling place of God in the Spirit, and into a royal priesthood and a holy nation; it is also a sacramental bond of unity linking all who are signed by it."[57]

Resurrection

The focus on the Resurrection in *Christian Initiation,* General Introduction, explains why the Church prefers to celebrate the Sacrament of Baptism at the Easter Vigil and on Sundays. Baptism is permitted on any day, but its meaning more clearly links to the Resurrection when it takes place on a Sunday and especially at the Easter Vigil. Baptism gives Christians a share in the Resurrection, making them partakers in the life of Christ, anticipating the hope of their own joyful resurrection to come. The Easter Vigil is therefore recommended first as the appropriate day for the Baptism of infants.[58]

The connection between Baptism and resurrection also explains why the Church permits—indeed, encourages—Baptism by immersion, not just

---

54. CI, 2.
55. For example, 1 John 3:1.
56. See Galatians 3:26 and Romans 8:14–17.
57. CI, 4.
58. See *Order of Baptism of Children* (OBC), 9.

This font was found under the nave of the Church of San Vitalis (modern-day Sbeitla, Tunisia). The font is most likely from the fourth century.

Baptism by pouring. Both options are always listed in this order: immersion or pouring.[59] The first option in liturgical rubrics is generally understood to be preferred. The *Catechism of the Catholic Church* explains this preference: "Baptism is performed in the most expressive way by triple immersion in the baptismal water."[60] *Christian Initiation,* General Introduction, states quite simply that Baptism by immersion "more suitably signifies participation in the Death and Resurrection of Christ."[61] The *Rite of Christian Initiation of Adults* holds that either immersion or pouring may be chosen, "whichever will serve in individual cases and in the various traditions and circumstances to ensure the clear understanding that this washing is not a mere purification rite but the sacrament of being joined to Christ."[62] The *National Statutes for the Catechumenate*, passed by the United States Conference of Catholic Bishops in 1986, says that immersion "is the fuller and more expressive sign of the sacrament and, therefore, provision should be made for its more frequent use in the baptism of adults."[63] So important is the Resurrection to Christian faith

---

59. See, for example, *Code of Canon Law* (CCL), 854.
60. CCC, 1239.
61. CI, 22.
62. *Rite of Christian Initiation of Adults* (RCIA), 213.
63. *National Statutes for the Catechumenate* (NSC), 17.

that the construction of church buildings in the United States should include baptismal fonts that permit immersion.[64]

Biblical testimony implies that the first Baptisms were done by immersion. St. Paul wrote that we are baptized into the death of Christ: "We were indeed buried with him through baptism into death, so that, just as Christ was raised from the dead by the glory of the Father, we too might live in newness of life."[65] A similar passage occurs in the Letter to the Colossians: "You were buried with him in baptism, in which you were also raised with him through faith in the power of God, who raised him from the dead."[66] Both of these passages come to life when one imagines the Apostles baptizing new believers by immersion in deep water.

Other passages make similar implications: 1 Peter 3:21 says that Noah's flood prefigured Baptism, an analogy that only makes sense if the practice at the time involved a life-threatening amount of water. Jesus describes Baptism as "being born of water and the Spirit,"[67] as if the quantity of water in Baptism resembled the enveloping water that accompanies childbirth. Those who were baptized "clothed" themselves in Christ,[68] which suggests that people entered the waters of Baptism naked, as they would enter a bath. All these passages support the argument that the Apostolic Church practiced Baptism by immersion because it helped make the connection between a person who dies to a former way of life in order to rise with Christ, just as Jesus died to his earthly life and rose from the dead.

> You were buried with him by baptism, in which you were also raised with him through faith in the power of God, who raised him from the dead.
>
> —Colossians 2:12

Limbo

Belief in Original Sin caused Catholics concern about the eternal salvation of those infants innocent of any personal wrongdoing who died before Baptism. As shown earlier, St. Augustine had taken the grim view that all those who die without Baptism suffer "eternal death." He thought that those responsible for their own personal sins would suffer worse than infants, who

---

64. See *Built of Living Stones: Art, Architecture, and Worship* (BLS), 69 §2.
65. Romans 6:4.
66. Colossians 2:12; see also 3:1–4.
67. John 3:5.
68. Galatians 3:27–28.

had never received the opportunity to make moral choices. However, dying without Baptism, in his view, could not offer eternal life. Augustine envisioned a different kind of eternal punishment, less severe than that of knowledgeable adults who made the personal choice not to be baptized.

Nonetheless, it is hard to imagine anyone more innocent than a baby. This led to a belief in a spiritual state called limbo, where God consigned children who died without Baptism through no fault of their own. The belief had been popular, but was never accepted as a doctrine of the Catholic Church. It was, at best, a theory to explain how God could balance the teachings of Jesus on the necessity of Baptism with the obvious innocence of very young children.

In 2007 Pope Benedict XVI received a report from the Vatican's International Theological Commission, hoping to put the matter to rest. After all, parents who lose a child suffer more than sufficient grief. The thought that they may not enjoy eternal life with their child imposes an even harsher, lasting spiritual burden. The commission's statement bore a positive title, *The Hope of Salvation for Infants Who Die without Being Baptized*. The commission could not escape the traditional theological challenge, but framed it within a more positive light: hope. In the concluding paragraph, the commission declares the Church's foundational belief as taught by Christ: "the ordinary way of salvation is by the sacrament of Baptism." However, the theological reflections on the practical matter of infant mortality "provide strong grounds for hope that God will save infants when we have not been able to do for them what we would have wished to do, namely, to baptize them into the faith and life of the church."[69]

The *Catechism of the Catholic Church* had already laid a similar foundation for hope:

> As regards *children who have died without Baptism*, the Church can only entrust them to the mercy of God, as she does in her funeral rites for them. Indeed, the great mercy of God who desires that all men should be saved, and Jesus' tenderness toward children which caused him to say: "Let the children come to me, do not hinder them," allow us to hope that there is a way of salvation for children who have died without Baptism. All the more urgent is the Church's call not to prevent little children coming to Christ through the gift of holy Baptism.[70]

---

69. *The Hope of Salvation for Infants Who Die without Being Baptized*, 103.
70. CCC, 1261; quoting Mark 10:14; see 1 Timothy 2:4.

Indeed the funeral rites revised after the Second Vatican Council include prayers for a child who dies before Baptism. They imply that because of the faith of the parents, the child has died within the embrace of the Church's care and hope for eternal life.

When to Baptize and the Role of Godparents

The Catholic Church encourages parents today to have their children baptized "in the first few weeks."[71] At the time that the post-Conciliar *Code of Canon Law* went into force (1983), this seemed to offer a generous concession. In the past, parents were urged to have their children baptized within the first few days after birth. Now they are given more time.

The short window stems from the concern about what happens to a child who dies before Baptism. The Church is far more confident at the unfortunate death of a child who has already been baptized. In the days of St. Augustine, when infant mortality was high, parents were urged to have infants baptized soon after birth while the children were still alive.

Today in the United States the infant mortality rate is fairly low. Parents assume that their newborns will live. Consequently, some parents have become complacent. Confident of the child's good health, no longer sensing the need for immediate Baptism, some parents delay not just days or weeks but months and years. Nonetheless, the encouragement of the Church remains strong: conduct the Baptism within the first few weeks after birth. Consequently, prior to the Council, a mother was often not present for the Baptism of her own child. She may still have been recuperating from childbirth.

Godparents, then, took a strong ritual role at the Baptism of children. In practice, they were the adults in the room. In the Hispanic community, for example, the bonds between godparents and parents have been and remain quite strong. The godparents' acceptance of the child in the moments after Baptism seals a relationship that is considered broadly familial.

The godparents are intended to represent the broader Christian community. Although parents customarily choose godparents from among their extended family members, the requirements for serving as a godparent make no mention of a family relationship. Instead, the Church has more concern that godparents be fully initiated, having received the Sacraments of Baptism, Confirmation, and Eucharist. They are also to lead "a life of faith in keeping with the function to be taken on," "not be bound by any canonical penalty,"

---

71. CCL, 867 §1.

Godparents are intended to represent the broader Christian community.

and "not be the father or mother of the one to be baptized."[72] Aunts and uncles, cousins, and even grandparents already have other responsibilities and relationships within the family. Godparents represent the entire Christian community. In practice, though, many parents want godparents within the family, and believe that they may especially provide assistance in nurturing their children's faith.

Although some people think a godparent should take complete responsibility for godchildren in the potential tragic circumstances in which they may be deprived of their parents, the official responsibilities for godparents have something else in mind. They do not replace parents who have died; they assist parents while they are alive.

A non-Catholic Christian may stand as a Christian witness together with one godparent from the Catholic Church. This role affirms the validity of Baptism in non-Catholic churches, builds bridges of ecumenism, and involves good models of Christian service from outside the full communion of the Catholic Church.

The Church recommends that the godparent at Baptism serve again as the godparent at Confirmation. This further demonstrates the enduring role that godparents accept. They remain active in the life of the child, encouraging religious formation and prompting participation in the sacraments of the Church.

---

72. CCL, 874 §1, 5°.

The Second Vatican Council, however, wanted parents to have a stronger role in the Baptism. This has been reflected in the revised rite. In practice, many parents still assume that godparents should hold the baby for the Baptism. The present ritual encourages parents to do so. They will be responsible for raising the child, including sharing the faith. Godparents share that responsibility; they do not replace it.

So important is the role of the believing parent that the *Order of Baptism of Children* makes a concession for any parent who does not share Christian faith. For example, a Catholic may be married to a non-Christian who holds no objection to the Baptism of the child. Such a parent "may remain silent" and is asked only to "provide for or at least permit the instruction of the child in the baptismal faith."[73]

Baptism presumes the faith and good intentions of at least one parent. Short of discerning that, the pastor may defer Baptism. Ordinarily, ministers cannot refuse sacraments "to those who seek them at appropriate times, are properly disposed, and are not prohibited by law from receiving them."[74] If there is no founded hope that the infant will be brought up in the Catholic religion, "the baptism is to be delayed"[75] These rules are aimed at ensuring the integrity of infant Baptism. The ceremony elicits several responses from parents and godparents about their intent to share faith with their children. The meaning of infant Baptism relies on the faith of the parents, and the faith of the parents implies their intention to share the Gospel with their children.

> The three Sacraments of Christian Initiation so work together that they bring to full stature the Christian faithful, who exercise in the Church and in the world the mission of the entire Christian people.
> —*Christian Initiation*, General Introduction, 2

Parents are thus urged to share their faith with the child from the first moment of the infant's life:

> The Church believes that there is nothing more ancient and nothing more proper for herself than to urge all—catechumens, parents of children who are to be baptized, and godparents—to that true and active faith by which, as they hold fast to Christ, they enter into or confirm the New Covenant.[76]

---

73. OBC, 5 §4.
74. CCL, 843 §1.
75. CCL, 868 §1, 2°.
76. CI, 3.

Preparing the Order of Baptism of Children

> "Parents and godparents,
> this light is entrusted to you to be kept burning brightly,
> so that your children, englightened by Christ,
> may walk always as children of the light
> and, persevering in the faith,
> may run to meet the Lord when he comes
> with all the Saints in the heavenly court."
>
> —*Order of Baptism of Children*, 64

The Baptism of children (or infants) is a joyful occasion for the entire parish community. Welcoming children into the Church is a moment of great festivity—not just for families but for all God's people. As children are reborn in the waters of Baptism, their initiation as members of the Body of Christ is the most important event of their lives. It is a moment in which they are sacramentally joined to Christ, who will lead and guide them as they follow their baptismal call to holiness throughout their lives. Baptism is a moment to be prepared and celebrated by all members of the community.

The Order of Baptism of Children

The primary ritual book used for baptizing children is the *Order of Baptism of Children*. This ritual was one of the first rites to be revised and translated into the English vernacular language following the reforms called for by the Second Vatican Council. Originally promulgated in 1969, the second edition of this ritual text was issued in 1973 in Latin. Following the new norms for translating ritual texts into vernacular languages according to the 2001 document, *Liturgiam authenticam*, the revised and retranslated ritual text for use in the diocese of the United States was approved by the Holy See on April 11, 2019. The United States Conference of Bishops decreed that the new ritual text may be used beginning on the Feast of the Presentation of the Lord, February 2, 2020. The mandated use is to be Easter Sunday, April 12, 2020. This ritual text, previously referred to as the *Rite of Baptism for Children*, is now the *Order of Baptism of Children*. This naming convention follows the Latin text and is consistent with the other revised translations promulgated following the 2011 third edition of *The Roman Missal* (i.e., *Order of Confirmation* and *Order of Celebrating Matrimony*).

Presiders and pastoral ministers will find little difference between the first and second editions in English. The revised translation continues to follow the same organizational structure with seven chapters and an appendix; it continues to incorporate the adaptations previously approved for use in the United States and the rubrics remain essentially the same. The major difference, are of course with wording and syntax, and the minor changes introduced with the Missal are now consistently updated within the revised ritual text.[1] The major changes include:

> The text of an optional introductory monition, the addition of a sample acclamation after each Baptism, harmonized rubrics incorporating previously approved U.S. ritual variations, the option to use an expanded Litany of the Saints, and a new appendix for the Baptism of children within Mass.[2]

The *Order of Baptism of Children* begins with two *praenotanda*, or introductory documents. While these *praenotanda* are not the ritual texts themselves, they are crucially important because they provide deeper theological, liturgical, ministerial, and logistical insight into the meaning of the rite and how it should be celebrated.

The first introduction, *Christian Initiation*, General Introduction, has a broad scope; it addresses the initiation of all who are being baptized, regardless of their age. It offers a theological foundation for understanding Baptism as the sacrament that initiates people as followers of Christ,[3] and it identifies the roles and requirements for godparents and the ministers of Baptism.[4] It then establishes norms that apply to all Baptisms: the use of clean, blessed water,[5] the option for immersion or pouring,[6] the proper formula for administering Baptism,[7] guidelines for locations[8] and times[9] of Baptism, and general

---

1. This includes an updated appendix with rubrics and texts for celebrating the Baptism of several children or one child during Mass. This is explained in more detail beginning on page 35.
2. *Newsletter* of the Committee on Divine Worship; May 2019; Volume LV.
3. See CI, 1–6.
4. See CI, 7–17.
5. See CI, 18–21.
6. See CI, 22.
7. See CI, 23.
8. See CI, 24–26.
9. See CI, 27–28.

permissions for adapting the rite.[10] This introduction addresses the Baptism of both children and adults, so it is found in both the *Order of Baptism of Children* and the *Rite of Christian Initiation of Adults*.[11]

The second introduction, the *Order of Baptism of Children: Introduction*, follows. This document provides more targeted guidelines that apply only to the Baptism of children, addressing the importance of baptizing them as infants[12] and the ministerial roles of parents and other members of the Church.[13] The document describes specifics about the time and place for Baptism to occur[14] and provides a summary of the structure of the various rites.[15] It concludes with two lists of permissible ritual adaptations that may be made either by conferences of bishops or by bishops[16] or by the minister of Baptism in a particular place.[17]

Immediately following the two introductions, the main body of the *Order of Baptism of Children* begins. It is divided into seven chapters. The first three chapters outline the primary rites for the Baptism of children:

- Chapter I: Order of Baptism for Several Children
- Chapter II: Order of Baptism for One Child
- Chapter III: Order of Baptism for a Large Number of Children

All of these rites presume the presence of an ordinary minister of Baptism (bishop, priest, or deacon) leading a communal celebration of the sacrament in an ordinary setting (church or baptistery with a font). The rites also presume that Baptism is being celebrated without Mass. Instructions for adapting the rites for use during Mass are included in the ritual introduction and in the newly added appendix.[18] The difference between "several children" and "a large number of children" is not specified in the text.

The next two chapters outline provisional rites that are used when a bishop, priest, or deacon is not available:

- Chapter IV: Order of Baptism of Children to Be Used by Catechists in the Absence of a Priest or Deacon

---

10. See CI, 30–35.
11. The *Rite of Christian Initiation of Adults,* or RCIA, is the ritual book that is used for initiating adults or children who have reached catechetical age.
12. See OBC, 1–3.
13. See OBC, 4–7.
14. See OBC, 8–14.
15. See OBC, 15–22.
16. See OBC, 23–26.
17. See OBC, 27–31.
18. See OBC, 29.

- Chapter V: Order of Baptism of Children in Danger of Death, or at the Point of Death, to Be Used in the Absence of a Priest or Deacon

As will be addressed later in this resource, both of these chapters omit specific texts and ritual actions reserved to ordained ministers. If a child is in danger of death, the rite requires only the minimum essentials: pouring water—even unblessed water—and saying the baptismal formula, preferably in the presence of at least one or two witnesses.

Chapter VI outlines the Order of Bringing a Baptized Child to the Church. This rite is intended to be used when a child who was baptized in danger of death or in other dire circumstances has survived. Baptism cannot be repeated and so this rite includes the components that were omitted during the child's actual Baptism. It is intended to be a full, joyful celebration of the baptized child's initiation. It may be celebrated only by an ordained minister of the sacrament—a bishop, priest, or deacon—and it may only be celebrated in a church.

Chapter VII includes various texts that may be used in the baptismal rites. This includes the readings from the Old Testament, New Testament, and Gospel accounts, Responsorial Psalms and Gospel acclamation verses, alternate formularies for the Prayer of the Faithful, alternate prayers of exorcism and blessing of water, numerous acclamations and hymns, and options for the final blessing at the conclusion of the rite. In the revised rite the Litany of Saints is included in this chapter (it was formerly in the appendix).

The most significant change to the *Order of Baptism of Children* concerns the appendix. In the previous edition, the celebration of Baptism at Mass, although permitted, did not receive a lot of attention. It was merely mentioned at paragraph 29 in the Introduction. Now, texts for use within Mass are included for the celebration of Baptism for several children and for one child. This is a welcome pastoral inclusion that makes this wonderful and communal option more accessible for pastors and parish communities.

Parish Preparation Team

The *Order of Baptism of Children* notes that those who are being baptized have "a right to the love and help of the community," and—consequently—the "People of God, that is the Church, represented by the local community, plays just as important a part in the Baptism of children as in that of adults."[19] Indeed, many members of the parish have roles to play:

- Bishops, priests, and deacons are the ordinary ministers who celebrate Baptism.
- Office administrators handle initial inquiries and recordkeeping.
- Catechists or teams of catechists (often married couples or deacons and their wives) lead baptismal preparation sessions, often collaboratively with the director of religious education.
- Parish liturgists coordinate the ritual celebration of the sacrament.
- Music directors oversee the preparation of ritual music.
- Other parish liturgical ministers—including sacristans, servers, ushers, and greeters—assist immediately before, during, and after Baptism.
- Individual musicians, teams of musicians, and readers participate during the baptismal liturgy.
- Maintenance staff or other volunteers may be responsible for the liturgical environment.
- Worship teams, ministry coordinators, and liturgy committees may also have various responsibilities.

With so many individuals handling a wide variety of roles, intentionally creating a parish baptismal team is most beneficial. Designating a specific team ensures that there will be collaboration among the various ministers as they prepare families for the celebration of Baptism. Such collaboration is important for logistical reasons (for example, to ensure that the rite is celebrated well; to prevent families from being given different information; to establish norms for twinned, merged, or clustered parishes). The involvement of a team can also help reduce the burdens on pastors, especially in smaller parishes with little—if any—full-time ministerial staff.

Most profoundly, though, preparation teams are important because by their existence, they manifest a great theological truth about the parish community and the Church as a whole. The children who are being baptized are not merely being initiated into a loosely affiliated group of individuals. Rather, they are becoming members of an authentic community in which all people share their gifts in service of their common faith. Collaborative

---

19. OBC, 4.

teams are living symbols of this shared faith, which is indeed the "common treasure . . . to the whole Church of Christ."[20]

According to the *Order of Baptism of Children*, the primary role of the preparation team before a Baptism occurs is to prepare the parents "to prepare themselves for an informed participation in the celebration by suitable means."[21] The team, therefore, needs to determine the nature of baptismal preparation for parents and, as appropriate, godparents. The rite suggests two main components of preparation: (1) providing "books, articles, and catechisms aimed at the family"[22] and (2) visits from the pastor or other parishioners for the purpose of "pastoral instructions and prayer in common."[23] Including both of these components ensures that baptismal preparation is more than simply a class or a series of classes conveying information;[24] it is also a time for evangelization and for meeting with and accompanying parents as they prepare to welcome a new member of their familial "domestic church."[25] To that end, prayer should be an essential component of these meetings. Ideally, this prayer will incorporate the Scripture passages (simply by reading them or as the basis for *lectio divina*), hymns, prayers, and other elements included in the *Order of Baptism of Children*, a possibility that the rite itself envisions:

> During the meetings at which the parents are prepared for the Baptism of their children, it is of great importance that the instructions be supported by prayers and the rites. For this purpose it may help to use the various elements that are provided in the Order of Baptism for the celebration of the word of God.[26]

The preparation team should also be available to walk through the ritual with the parents and godparents (in the same manner as a wedding rehearsal) so that they are familiar with what will take place, that they know the answers to the questions the priest will ask, and there will be no last-minute surprises. The rite stresses that "the ministry and duty of parents in the Baptism of children carry greater weight than the duty of godparents";[27] therefore, it is

---

20. OBC, 4.
21. OBC, 5 §1.
22. OBC, 5 §1.
23. OBC, 5 §1.
24. Parish preparation teams might try to avoid using the terms *class* or *classes* when advertising baptismal preparation. Instead, emphasize the spiritual formation that will take place.
25. *Lumen gentium* (LG), 11.
26. OBC, 27.
27. OBC, 5.

important that parish preparation teams help prepare them for the celebration and enable them to participate fully during the celebration.

When ministering to families whose child will be baptized alone (either at Mass or without of Mass), parish preparation teams will have more opportunities to engage the involvement of extended family members as liturgical ministers. It can be difficult to organize their involvement when more than one family is having their children baptized at a single liturgy. In these instances, it is better for parish teams to schedule parish liturgical ministers.

The preparation team should also discuss the many details that are involved in the celebration of Baptism. These include, but are not limited to:

- when and how often Baptism will be celebrated in the parish;
- where the Baptism will take place (font, baptistry, sanctuary);
- whether a separate font will be necessary;
- how processions will flow;
- where all who assemble will stand, sit, or kneel;
- whether Baptism will be given by immersion or pouring;
- what Scripture readings, prayer texts, and music will be selected;
- what the child will wear (naked or clothed; white clothing or not; whether the family or parish will provide the white garment; if Baptism is by immersion, what clothes are most appropriate);
- whether family members will serve in some ministerial roles (readers, servers, music) and if so, what practices or walk-throughs will be necessary;
- how the liturgical environment will be prepared;
- whether parish policy on taking photos and videos has been established;
- whether microphones or other amplification will be needed.

How often baptismal preparation teams meet should be determined by individual parishes. Whenever they meet, however, it is good to begin with a short prayer related to Baptism; perhaps by reading or doing a short *lectio divina* with one of the Scripture texts that are used in the rite, or else by renewing their own baptismal promises. Reflecting on the importance of their own Baptism helps all who are involved with baptismal preparation to fulfill their ministerial roles "with due dignity," while being "courteous and affable to everyone."[28]

---

28. OBC, 7 §2.

Smaller Parishes

Regardless of the size of your parish and its staff, the range of its resources, the nature of your preparation team, and the number of ministers and volunteers, you can celebrate the *Order of Baptism of Children* well. The rites themselves are intended to be used by the universal Church with parishes both large and small. This book is filled with suggestions that may seem beyond the realm of possibility, but do not be discouraged. By focusing on what is possible in your pastoral situation, preparing those elements with care, and celebrating with joy, your baptismal celebrations will be enriched. Every measure that goes into strengthening baptismal celebrations—however small it may seem—is well worth the the effort.

Familiarity with the Ritual Books and Church Documents

Parish preparation teams will need to be familiar with the ritual books and Church documents concerning the celebration of the Order of Baptism. As you will see, the *Order of Baptism of Children* allows for some customization and room for adaptation (that is, the selection of specific readings and music, the wording of some responses and acclamations, the addition of names to the Litany of the Saints, various options for some prayers, and more). Baptism should always be "celebrated with due dignity and . . . be accommodated, as far as possible, to the circumstances and wishes of the family."[29] To ensure a fitting celebration in your particular pastoral situation, you are encouraged to make full use of these adaptations and choices permitted by the rites—many of which will be discussed in the sections that follow.

That being said, the baptismal rites are liturgical rites of the universal Church. Those who are entrusted with the responsibility of preparing baptismal celebrations are called to be stewards of the liturgy. Consequently, apart from those adaptations that are permitted by the rite, nothing should be altered (by ad-libbing prescribed texts) or omitted (by skipping readings or other required elements). Our liturgical rites express our deepest beliefs as the Church, and together, we should do all we can to ensure that the rites are celebrated faithfully and well.

Most stand-alone editions of *Order of Baptism of Children* are designed to be all-inclusive; they include the contents listed above plus the Lectionary texts. However, other ritual books may be used in the celebration of Baptism

---

29. OBC, 7 §2.

for children. The *Lectionary for Mass: Volume IV* includes the prescribed Scripture readings for the ritual Mass (these same readings may also be used if Baptism takes place without Mass). If the ritual Mass is not used and the readings are those of the day, the weekday or Sunday Lectionary will be needed. The *Book of the Gospels* may also be used. The third edition of *The Roman Missal* includes two formularies (sets of prayers) for use when the ritual Mass is permitted.

In addition to the ritual books, parish preparation teams will need to be familiar with several catechetical and liturgical documents. Of course, the *Constitution on the Sacred Liturgy* lays the foundation for all post-Conciliar liturgical rites and liturgical documents. The *Catechism of the Catholic Church* includes a section exploring the theology of the sacrament. The *Catechism* does not include the actual ritual texts; however, it is a valuable reference for those studying the rite, for those who want to know the teaching of the Church on the sacrament, and for those who want to refresh their knowledge of the sacrament as part of their preparation and celebration.[30] Knowing of the existence of the *Code of Canon Law* (1983) and its baptismal regulations can also be helpful.[31] When considering how to prepare the liturgical environment for Baptism, a helpful starting point is *Built of Living Stones*, a 2000 document by the United States Conference of Catholic Bishops. This document is intended to be a guide for those who are building or renovating existing churches and it provides sound theological principles that are helpful for all who care for worship spaces—even those that have already been built.[32] *Sing to the Lord: Music in Divine Worship*, the 2007 document from the United States Conference of Catholic Bishops, provides direction to those preparing music for the celebration of the Sacred Liturgy according to the current liturgical books.[33] Although it is not necessary for the Baptism of infants, the *Rite of Christian Initiation for Adults* (RCIA) offers additional insight into the celebration of the sacraments of initiation.[34] Parish preparation teams will also want to familiarize themselves with the rites for emergencies, not only those

---

30. See CCC, 1212–1284.
31. See CCL, 849–878.
32. See BLS, 51, 66–69, 92, 94–95, 101, 110–111; see also page 119 concerning the liturgical environment.
33. See *Sing to the Lord: Music in Divine Worship*, 206–212.
34. The resources section of this book beginning on page 151 lists numerous other publications that guide parents, godparents, catechists, and other ministers as they prepare for Baptism.

found within the *Order of Baptism of Children*[35] but those within *Pastoral Care of the Sick: Rites of Anointing and Viaticum*[36] and the *Order of Confirmation*.[37]

In addition to having a thorough understanding of the *Order of Baptism of Children* and the other ritual books and Church documents, preparation teams should also be intimately familiar with any documents and preparatory materials that are given to parents and godparents. Teams also can fruitfully read and discuss additional texts about how to celebrate the rite, and they should review any local baptismal guidelines from their particular diocese.

Pastoral Issues

Proper Ministers of Baptism

As mentioned earlier, the celebration of the Sacrament of Baptism involves a variety of ministries from priest and deacon to catechists, parents, and family members. It is a time of celebration as the whole Church gathers to give thanks for the gift of new life and to welcome a child into the Body of Christ. Often, especially when Baptism is celebrated without Mass, those in attendance are unsure of their role in the celebration (that is, responding to the prayers, singing, standing, and kneeling). Since the presence of a participating assembly is vital to the liturgy, it is important to help them understand their role as sharers in the Priestly, Prophetic, and Kingly ministry of Christ.[38]

The *Order of Baptism of Children* highlights the role of the entire people of God in the celebration of Baptism. So, in some sense, the entire community takes on a ministerial role. However, the ordinary ministers of the sacrament, those who "act in the Church in the name of Christ,"[39] are bishops, priests, and deacons. Only in cases of necessity, with permission, may they baptize outside their territory.[40]

Both the *Order of Baptism of Children* and the *Code of Canon Law* prescribe who can baptize when an ordinary minister is unavailable. First, in cases of necessity, most often in emergencies, any layperson who has the proper intention can baptize. This is why formation of the faithful is

---

35. See chapter V in the OBC.
36. See *Pastoral Care of the Sick: Rites of Anointing and Viaticum* (PCS), 275–296.
37. See chapter IV in the *Order of Confirmation* (OC).
38. See *Lumen gentium* (LG), 31.
39. CI, 11 §1.
40. See CI, 11 §2 and 11 §3; CCL, 862.

Parish teams should ensure that parents, godparents, and their guests are able to participate in the ritual.

important. The bishop may also appoint catechists to fulfill this role.[41] The latter is not a common practice in the United States, but in mission territories, where there are few priests and deacons, this is a viable option to help the life of the parish to flourish and grow.[42]

Parents, of course, have a ministerial role. It is important that they are present for the Baptism of their child and they have "parts truly proper to them"[43] during the liturgy. Parish preparation teams should ensure that they are able to do so fully, consciously, and actively.[44] Specifically, parents are to listen to "the instructions of the celebrant," and participate in "the prayer which they make with the whole community of the faithful, [and] they perform a true ministry when: a) they ask publicly that the child be baptized; b) they sign the child on the forehead after the celebrant; c) they renounce Satan and make the Profession of Faith; d) they (the mother in particular) carry the infant to the font; e) they hold the lighted candle; f) they are blessed with the formulas especially intended for mothers and fathers."[45]

---

41. See CCL, 861 §2.
42. It is important to note that in extreme cases, even a non-Catholic or a non-Christian may baptize as long as they have the right intention.
43. OBC, 5 §3.
44. See CSL, 14.
45. OBC, 5 §3.

Other liturgical ministers will perform their respective roles in baptismal celebrations. Hospitality ministers (ushers and greeters) greet families and guests, direct them to where they need to go, and answer other questions. Sacristans and servers assist with retrieving and returning necessary items before, during, and after the Baptism. Musicians facilitate and encourage the singing of all who gather, and readers proclaim readings and intercessions. During Mass, extraordinary ministers of Holy Communion may assist with the distribution of the Eucharist. Generally, trained parish ministers are best suited to carry out these ministries; however, family members who belong to the parish and already participate in these various ministries can certainly be invited to serve for baptismal celebrations.

Requirements for Baptism

At the bare minimum, clean and "true water,"[46] the spoken Trinitarian baptismal formula ("**N.**, I BAPTIZE YOU IN THE NAME OF THE FATHER, AND OF THE SON, AND OF THE HOLY SPIRIT"), and the proper intention of the minister are all that is necessary for a valid Baptism.[47] If this is true, why does the Church provide such an involved rite? The celebration of the Order of Baptism invites the assembly to recall Christ's passion, death, and Resurrection through rich signs and symbols. Whether celebrated within or without Mass, the signs and symbols help to make clear what is happening in the rite—sharing in Christ's death and rising with him to new life as part of his Body, the Church. As a general rule, the full liturgy provided in the rite itself should be followed. From the Word of God proclaimed to the anointings, each moment of the baptismal liturgy invites the assembly to contemplate more fully the Paschal Mystery and their witness as disciples of Christ.

> [T]he rite of immersion, . . . more suitably signifies participation in the Death and Resurrection of Christ.
> —*Christian Initiation,* General Introduction, 22

True water can be sourced from "rivers, seas, lakes, rain, melted snow or ice, [and even] condensation."[48] It should be clean and sufficient for either immersion or pouring. True water cannot be made from saliva, tears, wine,

---

46. CCL, 849.
47. See CI, 18, 23; see also page 143.
48. John M. Huels. *The Pastoral Companion: A Canon Law Handbook for Catholic Ministry,* fourth edition (Montreal: Wilson & Lafleur, 2009), p. 40.

or similar liquids. Outside of Easter Time, the water is blessed within the rite.[49] During Easter Time, the water that is blessed at the Easter Vigil should be used in the celebration of the sacrament. In most parishes, this is not an issue since there is a permanent baptismal font in the church. If the "font" blessed at the Vigil is temporary, consider siphoning the water into a vessel where the water can be kept clean and used throughout the season. The waters of Easter signify a clear relationship between Baptism and participation in Christ's Paschal Mystery.

Children are baptized in one of two ways: immersion or pouring. If baptized by immersion, the minister totally immerses the child in the water. To do so, the minister can lower and raise the child's body from the water three times. He can also hold the child's body in the water and pour water over the child's head, allowing the water to drench the child as it cascades into the pool of water into the font. The word *baptism* (from the Greek word *baptizo*) means "to immerse," and both introductory documents found in the *Order of Baptism of Children* give preference for immersion. This type of Baptism is a more powerful and richer expression of the symbolic nature of the sacramental washing. Bathing in the water helps the Christian faithful to understand that Christ is truly washing us of sin and restoring us to life in him. The washing signifies death—that is, putting aside one's old self and being born again into new life in him.

Baptism by pouring (or infusion) is the second option. In this form of Baptism, the minister simply pours water over the child's head three times as he or she is held over the baptismal font. While this form is permitted and valid, this practice often involves a minimal amount of water and can ineffectively signify or communicate the reality of God's action in the sacrament. A minimalistic approach does not speak to God's awesome mercy and love present in the ritual action.

The child may be anointed twice during the rite: first with the oil of catechumens before the Baptism itself (this anointing is optional), and second with the oil of sacred chrism after the water bath (this anointing is required). It is best practice for the anointings to take place whenever possible; however, in cases of emergency when the oils are unavailable or time prohibits their use, the anointings may be omitted.[50]

---

49. See CI, 21.
50. See OBC, 51.

Time and Place for Baptism

When considering the time and place for Baptism, pastoral ministers should discern with the parents what is in the best interest of the family.[51] "Baptism [is] the door to life and to the kingdom,"[52] so careful considerations must be taken if Baptism is delayed beyond a few weeks. The rite suggests that Baptism should be celebrated "during the first weeks after the birth."[53] Because canon law requires that Baptism take place a few weeks after birth, it is best for parishes to provide formation and liturgy preparation opportunities for the parents (and godparents) during the pregnancy.

Baptism should only be delayed when parents have no intention to raise the child in the Catholic faith.[54] In this case, the parish community may choose to continue to visit with and accompany the family as a witness of the Risen Christ. Such visits are meant to show support and should be casual and friendly. The purpose of the visits should not be to convert or harass. Forming a welcoming and hospitable community may, in time, influence couples who have shied away from Baptism to return to their community of faith, but in the meantime, the Church continues to minister to the family as needed.

Baptism is an ecclesial event, an action of the Body of Christ. Therefore, when possible, Baptism should be celebrated during the Easter Vigil or on Sundays, the day the Church observes the Resurrection.[55] Sunday is the pinnacle of our week on which the Christian community recalls the life, death, and Resurrection of Christ. It is the day the Church recalls and honors God's gift of salvation. St. Justin Martyr in his *First Apology*, says:

> And we make an assembly together on Sunday, because it is the first day, on which God, having transformed the darkness and matter, made the world; and Jesus Christ our Savior rose from the dead the same day.[56]

Sunday after Sunday, in the celebration of the Eucharist, God's pilgrim people join their hearts and minds giving praise and thanksgiving to God.

---

51. See OBC, 8. If for some reason, the mother is unable to attend her child's Baptism, the mother is to be blessed according to the Order of Blessing a Mother after Childbirth as found in the *Book of Blessings*, chapter I; see also page 146.
52. CI, 3.
53. OBC, 8 §3 and See CCL, 867 §1.
54. See OBC, 8 §3 and CCL, 868 §1, 2°.
55. See CCL, 856 and OBC, 9.
56. Justin Martyr, *First Apology* 67:3–8, as printed in Paul Bradshaw, *Eucharistic Origins* (New York: Oxford University Press, 2004), p. 63.

"Sunday . . . is at the very heart of the Christian life"[57] and as "the fundamental feast day," it invites us to ponder the "resurrection as the beginning of a new creation."[58] This new creation revealed in Christ's Resurrection is what is revealed in Baptism and thus renewed in our weekly Eucharistic feast.

While Baptism is often celebrated outside of Mass, it can also be celebrated within Mass "so that the whole community may be able [to] take part in the rite and so that the connection between Baptism and the Most Holy Eucharist may stand out more clearly."[59] Celebrating Baptism during Mass enables the community to renew their baptismal commitment and to remember that they will accompany this child as he or she grows in faith. The liturgical rite, therefore, invites the community to ponder its role in living the Christian life:

> The Sunday assembly commits us therefore to an inner renewal of our baptismal promises, which are in a sense implicit in the recitation of the Creed, and are an explicit part of the liturgy of the Easter Vigil and whenever baptism is celebrated during Mass.[60]

If there is a pastoral advantage, a weekday Mass is possible as well, but this should be carefully discerned and prepared. Parishes should ensure that an assembly is present to show the ecclesial dimension of the sacrament. The so-called "private" Baptism should not be encouraged or promoted.

As with weddings, destination Baptisms have become popular, especially as people move more often. Parents often desire to have their child baptized at the parish where they grew up or at a parish in which their "favorite" priest or deacon ministers. Traveling to a different parish church may allow for greater participation of family and friends, especially if parents and grandparents are not able to travel. However, under normal circumstances, the proper place for Baptism is the parents' parish church. That location is most appropriate because the parish is where the child will be

> Sunday is the day above all other days that summons Christians to remember the salvation which was given to them in baptism and which has made them new in Christ. . . . The liturgy underscores this baptismal dimension of Sunday.
>
> —*Dies Domini*, 25

---

57. *Dies Domini* (DD), 7.
58. DD, 2; quoting CSL, 106; DD, 24.
59. OBC, 9.
60. DD, 41.

raised, and the parish community will both nurture the child's faith and foster a deep communion with Christ through the church.

If a child is in danger of death, Baptism should be administered according to the prescribed rite as soon as it is feasible. It is permissible to celebrate the shorter rite at a hospital if the longer rite is not timely and would not provide a positive pastoral response.

Order of Baptism of Children within Mass

The appendix of the newly translated *Order of Baptism of Children* includes two forms of the rite that take place within Mass: the first form is for use with several children and the second is for one child. The only difference between the two forms is number: Prayer texts and rubrics are written in the plural form for the first option and in the singular for the second.[61] The newly added appendix incorporates texts from the Missal and provides the proper accommodations so that the baptismal liturgy flows within the Mass. Pastoral notes precede the two forms of the rite.

It is fitting that the first form outlines and provides the text for the celebration of the rite for several children. When a child is baptized, he or she is initiated into a community of faith. Baptizing several children during the same liturgy clearly communicates this reality and allows for a richer celebration of the rite. Baptism is a time for the community to joyfully celebrate its life in Christ and rejoice at the initiation of its newest members.

When it is possible, consider celebrating a Baptism during the Sunday Mass. Doing so has the potential to evangelize, catechize, and renew the entire community while effectively using parish resources. Instead of scheduling three or five "private" Baptisms during one month, consider the impact on the community if the parish celebrated several Baptisms at once during Sunday Mass. The musicians and other ministers can be better prepared to use their gifts and energy wisely.[62]

---

61. There are very few differences between the two forms of celebrating Baptism during Mass. Because of the similarities, the forms of the rite are not discussed individually within this resource. Presiders and pastoral ministers should note that the only differences between the two forms are the singular and plural language and rubric adaptations. The Order of Baptism for Several Children also provides more pastoral guidance in the rubrics for the procession and the Baptism itself with a greater number of children. These adaptations are eliminated in the Order of Baptism for One Child. It is also clear that the latter rite envisions that one presider celebrate the ritual.

62. Pastoral ministers should note that the same guidelines apply when celebrating Baptism during a weekday Mass; although, Sunday remains the Church's preference.

As noted earlier, it is the Church's preference that Baptisms be celebrated on Sunday. However, in terms of within Mass, the Order of Baptism for Children states that "this should not happen too often."[63] What does that mean? Simply, every Sunday Mass ought not to include Baptism lest it come to be seen as a regular part of the liturgy. What "too often" means will vary from place to place, and it needs to be balanced with the rite's injunction that an infant should be baptized "during the first weeks after the birth."[64] In smaller parishes, celebrating Baptism shortly after babies are born still may only be once every few months. In larger parishes—and with the growing numbers of clustered and merged parishes—"too often" will have a different meaning. Regardless of the size of your parish, celebrating Baptism during Mass at regular intervals is often beneficial and formative for families, parish ministers, and the entire assembly. Your preparation team can determine when and how often is appropriate (once per month, once every two months, at certain Mass times, and so on).

When celebrated regularly without Mass, perhaps on a specific Sunday of each month, Baptism is most appropriately celebrated communally. The parish community is invited to attend, and parish liturgical ministers are scheduled to serve. Scheduling Baptisms to follow a weekend Mass emphasizes the connection between Baptism and Eucharist, especially considering most families will have attended Mass prior to the baptismal liturgy. Parishioners then see and hear the about-to-be-baptized babies, and after Mass some of the more extroverted parishioners may seek out members of the family so that they may share congratulatory remarks and see the baby. Occasionally, a few parishioners may even stay for the entire celebration (be sure to invite them). Even when Baptism occurs outside of Mass, it is still a public sacramental rite of the whole Church—of both the universal Church into which the child is being initiated and the parish family.

As you review the ritual text, notice the stational structure; the movement from one place to another during the different parts of the rite (from entrance of the church to the place for the Word to the baptismal font and to the altar). The stational nature of the baptismal rite helps the gathered community enter more fully into the Paschal Mystery and reflect on the pilgrim journey that commences at Baptism. Also, notice the rite's emphasis on the role of the community that gathers and accompanies the family. The community

---

63. OBC, 250.
64. OBC, 8 §3.

is an essential participating presence in the celebration of Baptism. Keen awareness of these two elements can have a profound impact on how your parish prepares for and celebrates the baptismal liturgy.[65]

Selection of Prayer Texts and Readings

When preparing to celebrate the baptismal liturgy during Mass, there are some details that need particular attention. The preparation team should decide if the proper or assigned Mass texts (Collect, Prayer over the Offerings, Prayer after Communion) and readings of the day will be used, or if those from the ritual Mass, "For the Conferral of Baptism," can be used instead. Each of these Masses has unique prayer texts and options for readings that help highlight the celebration of the sacrament or sacramental.[66] The ritual Mass for Baptism has two sets of prayers from which to choose and there are a number of options for readings found in both the *Order of Baptism of Children* and the *Lectionary for Mass*.

When preparing to celebrate Baptism at a Sunday or weekday Mass, the preparation team must be familiar with the rubrics determining if ritual Masses can be celebrated:

> When Baptism is conferred during Sunday Mass, the Mass of the day is said or, during the Sundays of Christmas Time or of Ordinary Time, or on weekdays, the Ritual Mass for the Conferral of Baptism is said. However, while Baptism may still be conferred during Mass, the Ritual Mass is prohibited on Sundays of Advent, Lent, and Easter, on Solemnities, on the days within the Octave of Easter, on the Commemoration of All the Faithful Departed (All Souls' Day), on Ash Wednesday, and during Holy Week.[67]

Parish preparation teams should also consult the table of liturgical days when determining levels of importance. This will help guide the decisions for when ritual Masses are permitted or prohibited.[68]

During **Advent**, the ritual Mass for Baptism is prohibited on Sundays. When Baptism is celebrated at Sunday Mass during Advent, the prayers and readings assigned for the day take precedence. The readings assigned to these

---

65. The stational nature and emphasis on the community is evident no matter what form of the rite is used.

66. For more detailed information on choosing a Mass (the prayers and readings) see chapters VII and VIII of the *General Instruction of the Roman Missal*, 352–385.

67. OBC, 252; see also GIRM, 372.

68. See the Table of Liturgical Days found at the end of the document *Universal Norms on the Liturgical Year and the General Roman Calendar* (UNLY).

four Sundays help the Church reflect on the coming of Christ at the end of time and at the Incarnation. If, after careful discernment, the preparation team decides that it would be of pastoral advantage, one reading may be substituted with a selection from the *Order of Baptism of Children*. If Baptism is celebrated on an Advent weekday, the ritual Mass is permitted, except if the day is ranked as a solemnity. In this case one reading may be substituted from the *Order of Baptism of Children*.

In the United States, the ritual Mass for Baptism may not be celebrated on the Sundays of **Christmas Time**. You may choose to use the readings assigned for the Sunday or those from the *Order of Baptism of Children*. If Baptism is celebrated on a Christmas weekday, the ritual Mass is permitted except if the day ranks as a solemnity. In this case one reading may be substituted from the *Order of Baptism of Children*.

During **Lent**, the ritual Mass for Baptism is prohibited on Sundays. If Baptism takes place during Sunday Mass, parish preparation teams must select the readings of the day. If Baptism is celebrated on a weekday during Lent, the ritual Mass is permitted, except if the day ranks as a solemnity. In this case one reading may be substituted from the *Order of Baptism of Children*.

During **Easter Time**, the ritual Mass for Baptism is prohibited on Sundays. The *Order of Baptism of Children* encourages parishes to celebrate Baptism at the Easter Vigil "to illustrate the paschal character."[69] The Vigil readings must be used and should not be replaced with readings from the *Order of Baptism of Children*. The readings assigned to the Sundays of Easter invite the Church to learn about the early community of Christians and about the activity of the resurrected Christ before his Ascension into heaven. If, after careful discernment, the preparation team decides that it would be of pastoral advantage, one reading may be substituted from the *Order of Baptism of Children*. Pastorally, this should be a rare occurrence and only permitted for significant need. If Baptism is celebrated on a weekday during Easter, the ritual Mass is permitted, except for if the day is ranked as a solemnity. In this case one reading may be substituted from the *Order of Baptism of Children*. During the Octave of Easter or another Easter weekday, if the parish hosts a mystagogical reflection on the Easter sacraments, you might consider celebrating a Mass with a Baptism if this seems appropriate.

During **Ordinary Time**, the ritual Mass for Baptism is permitted on Sundays. When preparing baptismal liturgies during Ordinary Time, first

---

69. OBC, 9 and 250.

consider the assigned readings. This honors the structure of the Lectionary and helps discern what will most benefit the gathered community. Often the readings during this season focus on discipleship and mission that are very appropriate for the celebration of Baptism and will engage the assembly in recalling their own commitment to proclaim the Gospel by the witness of their lives. The ritual Mass is permitted on weekdays in Ordinary Time except for if the day is ranked as a solemnity. In this case one reading may be substituted from the *Order of Baptism of Children*.

Baptisms may be celebrated on **Solemnities of the Lord and of the Saints**, but the ritual Mass for Baptism is prohibited. When Baptism is celebrated at Mass the prayers and readings assigned for the day take precedence. Such days include Mary, the Holy Mother of God; Ascension of the Lord; All Saints; St. John the Baptist; and the Assumption. Parents may wish to have their child baptized on these days because they have a particular devotion associated with the day or because the solemnity is important in the life of the parish. If, after careful discernment, the preparation team decides that it would be of pastoral advantage to schedule a Baptism on this day, one reading may be substituted with a selection from the *Order of Baptism of Children*. However, this substitution should be a rare pastoral occurrence and only permitted for significant need. Also ranking as a solemnity are those days proper to the local Church such as the anniversary of the dedication of the church, the title of one's church, and the title of the cathedral; therefore, the ritual Mass for Baptism would be prohibited on these days as well.

By celebrating **Feasts of the Lord and of the Saints** throughout the liturgical year, the Church proclaims Christ's Paschal Mystery. If a Baptism takes place on any feast, the ritual Mass is permitted. However, since these observances help unpack the richness of Christ's death and Resurrection, those preparing the liturgy should first consider celebrating the Mass of the day instead of the ritual Mass for Baptism.[70] The prayers and readings assigned to these days can help illuminate the mystery of Baptism and invite the assembly to reflect on a particular aspect of the Paschal Mystery as revealed in a particular feast. For

> Throughout the course of the year the Church unfolds the entire mystery of Christ and observes the birthdays of the Saints.
>
> —*Universal Norms on the Liturgical Year and the General Roman Calendar*, 1

---

70. See GIRM, 354 and 372.

example, on the Feast of the Exaltation of the Holy Cross, which occasionally falls on a Sunday, the homily can help the community focus on the power of the cross. This feast invites all the baptized, those washed in the waters of Baptism, to ponder the mystery of dying with Christ and rising to new life. It invites us to reflect on our role as disciples who are called to go forth and share the Good News to all peoples.

Both **Obligatory and Optional Memorials** fall on weekdays—never on a Sunday, for that day, as the high point of the week, takes precedence. The ritual Mass, "For the Conferral of Baptism," may be used on memorials, which means that the readings and prayers may be taken from the ritual Mass.[71]

It is important to remember that the Lectionary is arranged intentionally throughout the liturgical year and not according to "themes" (such as Catholic Schools Week, Diocesan Appeal). The readings for Sunday take precedence, especially because the First Reading and the Gospel are most often paired to complement each other. If, when allowed, a different reading or readings are chosen, consider changing the Second Reading so that the connection between the First Reading and the Gospel is maintained and the Second Reading conveys theological meaning on the Sacrament of Baptism. Use caution when selecting texts from the ritual Mass rather than the readings and prayers of the day. Doing so disrupts the semicontinuous nature of the day and a well-prepared homilist can easily connect these texts to the sacrament being celebrated, especially in terms of Christian discipleship. Whenever a parish preparation team and family members discern the possibility of selecting alternate readings, the following questions will be helpful in guiding their process:

- For what purpose are we changing the readings?
- Do these readings fully serve the community and the sacrament?
- What are we missing when choosing our "favorite" readings?

The Order of Celebration

Since both forms of the Order of Baptism of Children within Mass are essentially the same (except for the plural vs. singular forms of the text), the pastoral commentary that follows applies to both forms.

---

71. The only time there might be a restriction to this rule is if the saint that is celebrated is the patronal saint of the parish. In this case, the ranking is lifted from memorial to solemnity; therefore, the rules for a solemnity apply. Parish preparation teams should be aware that the same rules apply whenever Baptism is celebrated at Mass regardless of the number of children.

Introductory Rites

Outline of the Rite

- Rite of Receiving the Children/Child
  - [Song]
  - Gathering at doors of the church [or other place in church]
  - Sign of the Cross
  - Address to the parents and godparents
  - Questioning of the parents and godparents
  - Signing of the children's/child's forehead with the cross
- Procession to the Altar / Song
- Gloria
- Collect Prayer

Rite of Receiving the Children/Child

The previous *Rite of Baptism for Children* noted that when this rite is celebrated during Mass, the Rite of Reception altered the Introductory Rites—the Sign of the Cross, Greeting, and Penitential Act were omitted.[72] With the newly translated rite, when Baptism takes place at Mass, the greeting and the Penitential Act (including the Kyrie) continued to be omitted but the Sign of the Cross is offered and the Gloria is sung "when prescribed."[73] This has been clearly updated in the new *Order of Baptism of Children*.

The Rite of Receiving the Children emphasizes the community's hospitality, welcome, and willingness to accompany the parents and their children in their journey of faith as disciples of the Lord. The Christian community that receives children for Baptism boldly and joyfully proclaims its faith in Christ, which is why this rite should never be omitted or take place at another time apart from the baptismal liturgy.

The Rite of Receiving the Children continues to be organized into four parts:

- The Church, God's holy people, gathers.
- The priest celebrant warmly addresses the parents and godparents.[74]

---

72. See the 1969 edition of the *Rite of Baptism for Children*, 29 §1.
73. OBC, 251 §1 and 267.
74. A new addition to the Order of Baptism is the inclusion of a text used to address the parents and godparents.

- By means of questions, the parents, godparents, and the assembly declare their intentions and affirm their commitments to accompany the children in the faith.
- The priest celebrant, parents, and godparents trace the Sign of the Cross on the forehead of the children.

Although the Rite of Receiving the Children may take place at another location within the church, the Church's vision is that the children are received at the doors or entrance of the church. The location of this rite is significant for, again, it reflects both the welcoming and hospitable nature of the community and the children's entrance into the Body of Christ the Church:

> The reception of these children (as with adults in the Rite of Acceptance) takes place at the entrance or doorway of the church. At the threshold, we are invited into the church and into the house of the church. Here we will bless ourselves with the waters of baptism for years to come, to remember how God led us into the church through the saving waters.[75]

Immediately prior to beginning, a hospitality minister can lead the parents, children, and godparents to the entrance of the church and offer a few introductory remarks. First, that person should joyfully welcome everybody to the parish and to the church, particularly since so many people are guests. Second, that person can explain where to stand to permit maximum visibility, discuss any rules or guidelines for the use of photography and videography, and remind parents—if necessary—to ensure that their child's chest can easily be exposed for the pre-baptismal anointing. Third, if there will be processions, that person can also briefly mention that everybody will be moving from place to place during the rite. That person should invite the parents, godparents, and infants to arrange themselves appropriately. Finally, the hospitality minister can invite the assembly gathered in the church to stand and face the entrance of the church. Once all are gathered and all preliminary announcements are completed, the rite itself begins.[76]

---

75. Timothy Fitzgerald, *Infant Baptism: A Parish Celebration* (Chicago: Liturgy Training Publications, 1994), p. 34. It will be helpful to pastoral ministers to review the pastoral notes and ritual text for the Rite of Acceptance as found in the *Rite of Christian Initiation of Adults*.

76. When sacramental rites take place at Sunday Mass, there may be more people in attendance than usual. You will want to keep a prayerful tone in the church as people arrive for liturgy. Parish preparation teams can work with the music minister to prepare instrumental or choir prelude pieces to help minimize the conversation taking place in the church. Additional hospitality ministers can be scheduled to help guests find seats and bathrooms, answer questions, and distribute worship aids.

The rite begins with a psalm or another suitable song sung by the assembly as the ministers (priest celebrant and/or deacon, servers, readers) move to the entrance of the church or to the place where the parents and godparents are waiting. (Grandparents and other extended family or friends should already be seated in the pews. Bags, purses, and other belongings should be placed there prior to the start of the liturgy.) The priest celebrant and deacon should be fully vested (chasuble, dalmatic, and stole) for the celebration of Mass in the appropriate liturgical color of the day or season.[77] If the parents and godparents are stationed at the entrance of the church, be attentive to how they are arranged so the whole assembly can participate. The parents might hold their children and stand in the center of the group just inside the doors. The godparents can stand on either side of the parents. Liturgical ministers who take part in the entrance procession may stand to the side until the Rite of Receiving the Children is complete.[78] The assembly should be invited to stand and face the doors of the church so as to be engaged with the Rite of Receiving the Children.

> I have called you by name: you are mine.
> —Isaiah 43:1d

Once the ministers arrive and the music has ended, the priest celebrant makes the Sign of the Cross. The Greeting and Penitential Act are omitted. "Instead, the celebrant greets those present, especially the parents and godparents, recalling in a few words the joy with which the parents received their children as a gift from God, who is the source of all life and who now wishes to bestow his own life on them."[79] New to this translation is the inclusion of the words the priest may use to greet or address the parents and godparents. The priest celebrant may also write his own text or adapt what is provided so long as the meaning and the intent of the original text is preserved. The text provided in the rite is specifically addressed to the parents and godparents. It acknowledges the great joy their families are feeling at the birth of their children, emphasizes that this joy is shared by the Church, gives thanks to

---

77. OBC, 257 notes: "Meanwhile, the Priest celebrant, wearing vestments with the color proper to the day or the liturgical time, or with the color white or a festive color on days when Ritual Masses are permitted, goes with the ministers to the door of the church, or to that part of the church where the parents and godparents are gathered with those to be baptized."

78. If the parents and godparents are not greeted at the entrance of the church or nave, they are normally seated prior to the beginning of Mass near the sanctuary, preferably in the front pew. If this is the case, the Mass begins with the usual entrance procession and song.

79. OBC, 259.

When gathered at the back of the church for the entrance rite, invite the assembly to stand and turn to face that area of the church.

God for the Baptism that is to occur, and extends the Church's support as the parents and godparents raise their children in the Christian faith.

The priest celebrant then poses two questions to the parents. The rite provides two options. The first option is used when the number of candidates allows each set of parents to respond. The second option may be used when the number of candidates would unduly prolong this part of the rite. In this case, the priest celebrant asks each question once and then each family responds.

First, the priest celebrant asks, "What name do you give (or: have you given) your child?" The parents loudly say the name for the whole assembly to hear. Because God calls each of us by name and there is often a great deal of care that goes into the selection of a child's name, this is a significant moment in the rite. Even when many children are present, the priest celebrant can ask once: "What name do you give your child?" and each couple can respond in order. This naming does more than introduce the different children; it visibly manifests the Church as a gathering of families having come together as one Body to celebrate Baptism.[80]

The second question is, "What do you ask of God's Church for **N**.?" The routine response is "Baptism" or another general response. The rubrics provide for more robust possibilities: "the parents may use other words, e.g., *faith*

---

80. OBC, 260.

or the *grace of Christ* or *entry into the Church* or *Eternal life*."[81] During the parent's formation, catechists can help them discern a more personal response. Truly, what are these parents asking of the Church? This is a great opportunity to help personalize the liturgy. This type of personalization is not always permitted in the liturgical rites, but when the option is given, the ministers should take full advantage of the option and in this case, work with the parents to articulate what they are really seeking. For example, a couple might say, "We are are seeking new life in Christ for **N.** and the full support of this Christian community as we begin our journey together as a family." In this example, the couple has reflected on how they want to ask the community to walk with them and help them be good Christian parents. This response came out of a period of discernment and conversation with the preparation team and their family. When there is an especially large number of children, the best response for a group of parents may simply be "Baptism" or one of the other choices listed in the rite (such as "faith," "the grace of Christ," "entry into the Church," "Eternal life"). Asking this question once of all gathered parents can reduce nervousness and facilitate a strong, loud, unified response.[82]

Next, the priest celebrant addresses the parents, either with the text provided in the rite or in his own words, and helps them understand their responsibility in forming their child in the practice of the Catholic faith. If the priest celebrant decides to use his own words, they must be carefully crafted, theologically sound, and rehearsed. The ritual text can help the priest celebrant understand the Church's vision for this part of the rite. He will want to emphasize the importance of the domestic Church and the parent's role in passing on the faith. The parents respond to this question with a confident and loud "We do." Hopefully, this question has been thoroughly examined during the time of formation so the parents can honestly respond and understand this responsibility.[83]

The priest celebrant then questions the godparents about their readiness to assist the parents in their duties of raising the child in the Catholic faith. This is a rather sparse part of the rite, but during the time of formation, this question should be unpacked for the godparents so they can more fully understand their responsibility of nurturing the faith of the child and supporting the parents throughout the child's life.

---

81. OBC, 260; emphasis added.
82. OBC, 260.
83. See OBC, 262.

For questions that require an affirmative response, the priest celebrant may wish to remind the parents and godparents of the wording prior to asking the question ("We do/We are"[84]). Doing so ensures a strong, unified response rather than a mumbled, disparate mix of other replies ("Yes" or "Yeah" or "I do"). Because the parents and godparents are responding to these questions, consider having one of the servers hold a microphone so that the whole assembly can hear. When people are nervous and not used to speaking in front of people they may be reserved and quiet, even if they have practiced.

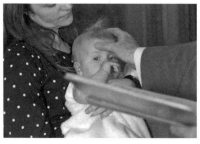

After the Signing of the Cross, the procession moves to the altar just as during Sunday Mass.

When the questioning is complete, the priest celebrant silently traces the Sign of the Cross on each child's forehead. This visually announces that each child has been claimed for Christ. He also invites the parents and, if appropriate, the godparents to do the same. The signing of the children's foreheads with the cross is the climax of the Rite of Receiving the Children, because the assembly, who has signed itself with this same cross countless times, is now handing on their story of salvation and the power of the cross to a new person of the faith. It is Christ himself who is present in this action and who will strengthen the children in their journey of Christian discipleship and faith.

After the signing with the cross, the procession to the altar takes place just as at a regular Sunday Mass except for the inclusion of the families and children. The singing of a song accompanies this action. This song should be familiar and may highlight the Paschal Mystery, new life, Baptism, or themes from the Scripture readings. The rite suggests verses from Psalm 84 (85).[85]

Carefully prepare how the ministers, parents, and godparents will move within the space. Without careful preparation, the rite may seem clumsy and undervalued, which prevents the assembly from fully participating and understanding the importance of this rite for the life of Christian faith. The liturgical procession helps the assembly to fully, actively, and consciously engage with the celebration and it is also a fuller witness to our earthly pilgrimage as we journey. To omit the procession (which is not an option) because

---

84. OBC, 263.
85. See OBC, 265.

it prolongs the liturgy sells the rite short and misses the potential to catechize the faithful and embody the faith.

The order of the entrance procession might look like this:

- [Thurifer with incense]
- Cross bearer
- Candle bearers
- Godparents, parents, and children (ordered by family)
- [Other ministers]
- Deacon carrying the *Book of the Gospels*[86]
- [Concelebrating priests]
- Priest celebrant

Pews for each family should be reserved near the front of the nave, near the ambo and altar. Parents, children, and godparents should process directly to those pews. Of course, the placement of families will vary for each community so the preparation team must consider a place where the families can fully and actively participate in the liturgy.[87]

The Penitential Act is omitted, and the celebration of the Mass continues with the Gloria (except during Advent or Lent), the Collect of the day or the ritual Mass,[88] and all are seated for the Liturgy of the Word. The Collect that is found in the rite itself is only used if a ritual Mass is permitted (outside of a Sunday, solemnity, or feast of the Lord).

The rite suggests that the children to be baptized may be carried to a separate place until the end of the Liturgy of the Word.[89] The introduction to the *Order of Baptism of Children* uses even stronger language:

> While the Liturgy of the Word is celebrated, it is desirable that children should be taken to a separate place. But care should be taken that the parents

---

86. If there is no deacon assisting Mass, then a reader may carry in the *Book of the Gospels*.

87. If the family has been received and welcomed at their seats, the entrance procession would have already taken place, so the ministers simply proceed to their places in the sanctuary.

88. The Collect, or the opening prayer, is a prayer addressed to God and prayed by the priest celebrant on behalf of the whole assembly. The priest celebrant invites the community to pray, during which each person silently prays and offers an intention (for example, for a sick family member, for peace and unity). After a period of silence, the priest then "collects" all those unspoken prayers and offers them to God, through Christ, in the power of the Spirit. The prayer concludes with the assembly's affirmation in a robust "amen." If Baptism is celebrated during a weekday Mass, the Collect of the day may be used.

89. See OBC, 264.

and godparents attend the Liturgy of the Word; the children should therefore be entrusted to the care of others.[90]

In theory, this enables the parents and godparents to focus on the reading(s) and homily with fewer distractions. However, the disadvantages are many. First, the children may not wish to go and may cause more disruption when taken from their parents and godparents. Second, without Mass, there is often no nursery or cryroom (or other place) for the children and caregivers to go. Third, as many new parents can attest, the parents may be more distracted by worrying about their baby than they would be if their children were with them.

In recent years, Pope Francis has spoken about the importance of parents bringing their children to Mass. In a homily given at the Sistine Chapel on the Feast of the Baptism of the Lord, Francis said:

> Today the choir sings, but the most beautiful choir is the children making noise. . . . Some of them will cry, because they are uncomfortable or because they are hungry: if they are hungry, mothers, feed them with ease, because they are the most important ones here.[91]

Moreover, it is incongruous to remove the children who are being baptized during the sacramental celebration of their own Baptism. Ideally, the parents with their children and godparents should remain in the church to hear the Word proclaimed. The children may need to be removed for feeding, fussiness, or changing.

Liturgy of the Word

Outline of the Rite
- First Reading
- Responsorial Psalm
- [Second Reading[92]]
- Gospel Acclamation
- Gospel

---

90. OBC, 14.

91. Pope Francis, "Homily for the Feast of the Baptism of the Lord: Mass and Administration of the Sacrament of Baptism," http://w2.vatican.va/content/francesco/en/homilies/2014/documents/papa-francesco_20140112_omelia-battesimo.html; accessed on July 30, 2017.

92. In most celebrations of the Mass taking place on weekdays (except for solemnities and feasts) there is no Second Reading.

- Homily
- Universal Prayer (or Prayer of the Faithful) and Litany of Saints
- Prayer of Exorcism and Anointing before Baptism
- Procession to the place of baptism [with song]

St. Paul tells us, "Faith comes from what is heard, and what is heard comes through the word of Christ."[93] As with any celebration of the sacraments, the Word of God is proclaimed before it is celebrated in order to form the assembly in faith and rouse their hearts to be missionary disciples. For example, if one reviews the *Rite of Christian Initiation of Adults*, we see that during the Period of the Catechumenate celebrations of the Word are encouraged to take place frequently so that catechumens might grow in holiness and come to embody the Christian story.[94]

In the case of infant Baptism, the proclamation of the Word is primarily for the gathered assembly and not the children. It is the assembly who is shaped and transformed by God's Word. They have just committed to accompanying these children as they grow in faith and now the assembly hears that story proclaimed once again. "The sacred celebration of the Word of God is intended to stir up the faith of the parents and godparents and others present, and to encourage them to pray together for the fruits of the Sacrament, before the sacramental action."[95]

The Liturgy of the Word follows the usual structure. Whenever the Word is proclaimed it should be done with great care and dignity. The proper ritual books should be used and those who proclaim the Word should be properly prepared and trained. Be sure to mark the appropriate readings with the included ribbons. If the Lectionary or *Order of Baptism of Children* seems too complicated to use, use dignified ritual binders; never proclaim from loose sheets of paper. Family members or friends of the family may be selected to proclaim the readings, but parish preparation teams should take the time to meet with them before the liturgy so that they can be familiar with the Lectionary, rehearse the texts, and understand parish practice. When Baptism takes place at Sunday Mass, it is probably best to schedule the usual parish ministers. It is the Church's preference that the Responsorial Psalm be sung and proclaimed from the ambo; this practice should not be changed for ritual Masses.

---

93. Romans 10:17.
94. See RCIA, 79.
95. OBC, 17.

For more solemn celebrations, especially during Sunday Masses, parish preparation teams might consider using the *Book of the Gospels,* especially if this is the norm for parish Sunday Masses. This ritual book can be carried by the deacon (or, in his absence, a reader) in the entrance procession and laid flat upon the altar until the Gospel acclamation. At that time, the deacon (or, in his absence, the priest celebrant) carries this ritual book in procession to the ambo accompanied by two candle-bearers while the acclamation is sung. The book is incensed and then the Gospel is proclaimed.

Homily

Following the readings, "the celebrant preaches the Homily, which is based on the sacred text, but should take into consideration the Baptism being celebrated."[96] The homily should not only break open the Scriptures, but also break open the mystery of Baptism, especially the responsibilities of the parents, godparents, and the whole Christian community as well as the meaning of discipleship. The homilist might take a cue from early Christian preachers like St. John Chrysostom and St. Ambrose and prepare a mystagogical homily. This form of preaching provides the opportunity for the homilist to use the rite and help "break open" the mysteries of Baptism. Helping the assembly ponder their experiences can only enrich the liturgical celebration and make it relevant within the life of the parish. Might the assembly be roused from their pews and embrace being missionary disciples?

After the homily, the assembly observes a period of silence. The other forms of the Order of Baptism (without Mass) provide some suggested texts for an optional song following the homily, but this is not an option during Mass.

Normally, the Creed is recited after the homily and before the Universal Prayer at Sunday Mass (and on solemnities), but since the entire community will make a Profession of Faith later, it is omitted here.

Universal Prayer (or Prayer of the Faithful) and the Litany of Saints

Following the homily and period of silence, the priest celebrant invites the assembly to stand and offer their prayers to God. The intercessions are the prayers that the Body of Christ, the baptized, offer on behalf of the community and world. If a deacon is assisting with Mass, he is the proper minister to offer the Universal Prayer or Prayer of the Faithful with the assembly responding. He may offer them from the ambo or his chair.[97] If there is no

---

96. OBC, 270.
97. See GIRM, 71.

A member of the parish staff might meet with the parents to discern what prayer texts and Scripture accounts will be used.

deacon, then a lay minister approaches the ambo to offer the prayers. The lay minister may be a parish minister (reader) or may be selected by the family. In either case, he or she must be properly prepared to speak (or sing) prayerfully from the ambo. However, for Sunday Masses it will probably be best for a parish liturgical minister to be scheduled. Keep in mind family members who are also members of the parish and are routinely scheduled as liturgical ministers. It is very appropriate for them to be scheduled today. If a family member or friend who is not a member of the parish is allowed to minister, parish preparation teams should take time before the liturgy to rehearse the prayers at the ambo so the minister is familiar and comfortable with the sound system and the texts.

The texts that are used for the Universal Prayer may be those found in the rite. However, the rite does allow new petitions to be added. When writing additional petitions it would be best to follow those norms provided by the *General Instruction of the Roman Missal*. Petitions are required for the Church, the world, the oppressed, and the local community.[98] The intercessions provided in the rite are addressed to Christ and speak to and pray for the parents, godparents, the children, the family, and the whole Christian people.

The preparation team might consider discerning with the parents what other intentions need to be offered, not only for the children and families but

---

98. See GIRM, 70.

also for the needs of the local community and other global needs. This provides an opportunity to engage the parents in a process of theological reflection upon baptismal discipleship during the formation process. This has the potential to expose the parents to see the needs of the world beyond where they live (for example, poverty, economic injustice) and to reflect upon what Baptism asks of everyone who is washed in the waters of rebirth. Petitions for family members who are ill or who recently passed away may also be added. The *Order of Baptism of Children* notes that if the mother died at childbirth, her name should be added to the Universal Prayer.[99]

Note that the Order of Baptism for Children does not include the familiar call to prayer, "We pray" or "We [Let us] pray to the Lord." Instead, the petitions are prayed and the assembly immediately responds with "Lord, we ask you, hear our prayer." Because this may be an unfamiliar pattern, it might be best to deviate from what is provided in the ritual text and add after each petition the familiar call to prayer. The assembly can then repond with either "Lord, hear our prayer" or what is provided in the ritual text. Parish teams might consider singing the petitions or at least the response. Appendix I in *The Roman Missal* provides sample chant tones for the Universal Prayer, or another musical setting can be used. Whatever the response, it should be specified prior to the petitions ("The response is . . .") or clearly noted in the worship aid so that all may respond accordingly without any awkwardness. If the response is to be chanted, the intercessions may be read by an assisting minister with the celebrant or deacon chanting "We pray to the Lord" or another invocation.

The Litany of the Saints, a deeply loved and familiar prayer of the Church, immediately follows the Universal Prayer. It is a sung prayer, led by two cantors or even a schola. Through this prayer, the assembly in their response, "pray for us," asks the saints to join the prayer of the community that these children may be filled with the Holy Spirit and joined to Christ's Body at Baptism. Baptism is truly a celebration for the entire Church—on earth and in heaven—who praises God for the gift of life.

---

99. See OBC, 31 §1. The rite also notes that "this should be taken into account in the opening instruction . . . and in the final blessing." If the mother is unable to attend the child's Baptism due to a difficult delivery or health issues, her needs (with her permission) could also be added to the Universal Prayer. Pastoral ministers should be aware of the Order of Blessing of Mothers after Childbirth, which is to be used only if mothers are unable to be present at their child's Baptism due to health issues. It is found in chapter I of the *Book of Blessings*.

The *Order of Baptism of Children* intends that the Litany of the Saints flows directly from the petitions and concludes the Universal Prayer, thus replacing the usual concluding prayer.[100] Notice that in the ritual text itself the litany is clearly part of the Universal Prayer; it does not include its own heading in the ritual text. The rite specifies that the priest celebrant invites the community to invoke the saints, but it does not provide a text for him to use. However, since the litany is part of the Universal Prayer, then it makes pastoral sense that the cantor should begin the litany with "Holy Mary, Mother of God" immediately following the last petition without an introduction from the priest celebrant. This enables a seamless, ritual flow.

It might be challenging for the community to know what is taking place since this is not the usual pattern for the Universal Prayer at Mass. If the priest celebrant desires to invite the community to pray the Litany of Saints as advised by the ritual text, he might consider taking a cue from the *Rite of Christian Initiation of Adults* that provides an introduction for the litany when prayed at the Easter Vigil.[101] Although this text is a bit lengthy, he may adapt the text to meet the needs of infant Baptism and the gathered assembly

This form of the Litany of Saints does not include the Kyrie. Also notice that the two forms of the Order of Baptism within Mass only include four invocations in the ritual text. The names of the saints provided in the rite are those who must be invoked; this does not mean, however, that only Mary, St. John the Baptist, St. Joseph, and Sts. Peter and Paul are to be invoked. In fact, the rite suggests, it is appropriate to add other saints' names to the litany, particularly the patrons of the children to be baptized and those of the parish. Depending upon the number of children being baptized, it may also be fitting to include the patron saints of parents, godparents, and even siblings. Consider adding other names, as the rite suggests, for this prayer to be more effective. A longer form of the Litany of Saints is provided in chapter VII of the ritual text. Without a longer litany, it is difficult for the assembly to enter into the rhythm of the prayer. The traditional chant may be the most widely known, but if your parish is familiar with another musical setting, consider what is most pastorally appropriate for your situation. Whatever setting is chosen should be familiar to parishioners, easily learned by those who do not know it, and able to be led competently by the musicians who are present.

---

100. See OBC, 272–273.
101. See RCIA, 220.

If for some reason, as was noted earlier, the children were taken out of the liturgy, they are returned to their parents while the litany is sung.[102]

Prayer of Exorcism and Anointing before Baptism

The Prayer of Exorcism and the Anointing before Baptism with the oil of catechumens follows the Litany of Saints and concludes the Liturgy of the Word. When the parents and assembly hear or see the word *exorcism*, demonic images from movies or books may flood their imagination. These scripted narratives and images distort and misrepresent the nature and purpose of an exorcism. During their formation, it is essential to help parents and godparents understand the beauty and purpose of the Prayer of Exorcism.

There is a difference between a major exorcism and a minor exorcism. A major exorcism is a completely separate rite of the Church and is used solely in situations that the Church has determined to be cases of demonic possession. In a major exorcism, a specific demon is addressed and expelled. The exorcism that takes place in the Order of Baptism is a minor exoricism. A minor exoricism is for the unbaptized and is a sign of the redemptive mission of Christ. This exorcism mirrors the minor exorcisms that are celebrated during the Period of the Catechumenate.[103] In a sense, the children are going through a mini-catechumenate. As adult catechumens participate in the rites of Christian initiation, minor exorcisms are celebrated throughout the year within a Liturgy of the Word as a powerful tool for the parish community to gather and reflect on sin and God's liberating love. If your community has a year-round process for Christian initiation, celebrating these minor rites communally could effectively catechize the community about God's power over sin and death. It will help "train" those who will eventually seek the Sacrament of Baptism for their children.

For the Baptism of children, the Prayer of Exorcism and Anointing before Baptism takes place in the sanctuary area and the procession to the font follows (unlike during the initiation of adults at the Easter Vigil in which the Litany of the Saints accompanies the procession to the font). The parents and godparents may remain in their pew as the priest celebrant approaches them, or they may stand in the center aisle facing the assembly so that all can visually participate. This clearly marks the distinction between the Liturgy of the Word and the celebration of the Sacrament of Baptism. Too often, this

---

102. See OBC, 273.
103. See RCIA, 90–94.

part of the liturgy is understood to be the beginning of the sacramental rite itself. This prayer and anointing helps prepare the children to enter the water-bath and receive the gift of new life.

The two options for the Prayer of Exorcism provide rich material for parents, godparents, and the whole Christian community to reflect on the reality of sin in the world. First, the prayers acknowledge God's saving action of sending Jesus to save the world from the darkness of sin. Second, the prayers identify Christ's triumph over sin and death, and the community asks for the strength of the Resurrection to accompany them on life's journey and for God to set his children free from sin and send the Holy Spirit upon them. These prayers do not shy away from confirming that evil is present in the world and that all people struggle between darkness and light. Before Baptism, we are more susceptible to the temptations of the world. Through Baptism, the power of Christ strengthens us to resist all that tempts us from God.

After the Prayer of Exorcism, the priest celebrant continues with a short prayer revealing to the assembly that the children are being anointed with "the oil of salvation / same Christ our Lord."[104] After this prayer, each child is anointed on the chest with the oil of catechumens. If there are a large number of children to be baptized (and other ordained ministers are present) the anointing may be done by several ministers.[105] This anointing speaks most powerfully when the priest uses a significant amount of oil (more than a drop or two) and applies it to the chest in the shape of a cross. To allow the symbol to speak most powerfully, the oil should remain on the children's chests; it should not be removed or wiped immediately with a towel or purificator.

Depending on the size of the group, the priest celebrant may consider saying this prayer for each child *while* he anoints. This adaptation may help draw out the richness of the prayer and help the assembly to connect to the rite. Parents may need to be reminded that, if the children are already clothed in the baptismal garments, the garments need to be loose around the neck so the minister can anoint the children's chests. Ideally, the children would either be naked and wrapped in a towel or dressed in simple garments that will be removed before or right after the immersion or pouring of water.

As this is the first of two anointings, it may also be pastorally advisable for the minister to say a few words about the oil that will be used. Many who are gathered will not necessarily distinguish between the chrism and the oil of

---

104. OBC, 275.
105. See OBC, 275.

catechumens, so a few well-chosen words of introduction can be a fine way to distinguish this anointing from the later anointing with chrism. The priest celebrant might integrate the historical origins of the oil. As Paul Turner writes:

> Traditionally, this represented a protective oil, like a sunscreen if you will, to reinforce the prayers of exorcism and keep away every evil influence from those who would now devote their lives to Christ.[106]

The *Order of Baptism of Children* provides the option for priest celebrants in the dioceses in the United States to omit this anointing if they do not find it to be "pastorally necessary or desirable."[107] Pastors and parish preparation teams should have a conversation about this rubric and have some idea what "pastorally necessary or desirable" means and how and when it may be applicable. For example, the anointing could be omitted because a child has an allergy to the oil or developed another skin trauma following birth. However, the anointing should never be omitted simply to save time or because it can be messy, especially when the oil is applied generously. If the anointing is omitted, the priest celebrant offers a shorter prayer that Christ strengthen the child, and then he lays "his hand on each child in silence."[108] The priest does not lay his hand on a child who was anointed.

Procession to the Font

The anointing (or laying on of his hand) concludes the Liturgy of the Word and the community now transitions into the celebration of the sacrament itself. The transition is marked by the procession to the baptismal font.[109] The vision of the rite is to process physically to the place where the Baptism will take place. This strengthens the image that we are a pilgrim Church on a journey. There are three scenarios presented in the ritual.

- First, the whole assembly processes to the font if it is located outside of the church. The rite presumes the whole assembly will participate in the liturgy so they accompany the family to the place for Baptism. The assembly should be able to see what is taking place and fully engage with the rite. Even if the font is not outside the church, but in an area that can accommodate the whole congregation (such as the narthex or main

---

106. Paul Turner, *Your Child's Baptism* (Chicago: Liturgy Training Publications, 1999), p. 22.
107. OBC, 276.
108. OBC, 276.
109. See OBC, 277.

entrance), the preparation team should consider how the congregation will form the procession and what path will be taken to the font.

- Second, if the font is in a place that is visible to the entire congregation, there is no reason for the entire assembly to take part in the procession. In this case, only the parents, godparents, priest celebrant, and necessary ministers (such as an altar server to hold the ritual book) process to the font. This may be adapted according to your individual space. If family and/or close friends are invited to process to the font, be sure that they do not obstruct the assembly's view of the font. If the area is large enough, consider inviting other baptized children to come forward to the font so that they can see what is taking place. Remember, processions help us contemplate our journey in this life and have great sign value to help the assembly embody the prayer.

- The third option suggests that if the area for Baptism is too small to accommodate the congregation, it may be celebrated at a more convenient place. In older churches that do not have a large font or separate area for Baptism, this is probably a familiar scenario. In this case, the community will need to purchase a beautiful and worthy vessel that can be easily placed in the sanctuary or somewhere in the nave for the celebration of Baptism. Some older churches maintain their original fonts, which were tall and slender pedestals that were rolled out of a niche for the celebration of the rite. The Church envisions that the rite be celebrated with the entire assembly participating, so this must be the goal for the parish preparation team and the font must be prepared accordingly.

When Baptism is celebrated outside of Easter Time, the Paschal candle is normally placed near the font. During Easter Time, the Paschal candle is normally near the ambo or altar and so the deacon or another minister (altar server) will need to carry the candle and lead the assembly members in procession to the font. The candle is then placed near the baptismal font.[110] A stand should be readied before the liturgy begins.

A communal song is sung while the assembly processes to the font. The rite recommends the singing of Psalm 23 (22), although other psalms, such as 27, 34, or 148–150 may be selected (or even another appropriate song). Psalms are appropriate choices for processional movements because they provide a

---

110. If your community is unfamiliar with processions of this nature, help them practice by incorporating processions in other liturgies such as the Rite of Acceptance into the Order of Catechumens, Presentation of the Lord, Palm Sunday, Corpus Christi, and the transfer of the Eucharist at the Evening Mass of the Lord's Supper on Holy Thursday.

Family and friends may gather near the font.

simple refrain that is easy for the assembly to remember and participate while moving and may not require a worship aid.

Once the ministers, parents, godparents, family, friends, and the parish community have gathered at the font, a server or another minister can help the faithful situate themselves so that they are able to participate in the celebration. A server or another minister can assist in arranging the community so that all are able to see and participate in the celebration. Consider inviting children to come closer to the font so that they can see what is taking place more easily. The parish preparation team must consider the space and how it will best accommodate the needs of the assembly gathered around the font. Hospitality ministers can also assist with helping people fill the space. The parish preparation team will need to decide whether the assembly will surround the font while the family stands in the middle or whether the assembly will stand on one side while the family is on the opposite side.

Celebration of Baptism

Outline of the Rite

- Blessing and invocation of God over the water
- Renunciation of Sin and Profession of Faith
- Baptism by immersion or pouring
- [Acclamation]
- Explanatory rites[111]

After the procession to the baptismal font, the priest celebrant invites the assembly to pray by reminding them of God's wondrous work in washing humanity "clean through the Sacrament of Baptism."[112] The priest celebrant can adapt the text that is provided in the ritual. If the text is adapted, the invitation should conclude with a clear statement of what is about to happen; for example: "And so, we now bless the water that will be used to baptize these children."

The rite provides three formulas for the blessing and invocation, although only the first option is provided in the texts for the celebration of Mass (the other two are in chapter VII). Each reveals aspects of salvation history. Option 1 addresses God and acknowledges his saving actions throughout history (Red Sea, Jordan River), which moves us to offer thanksgiving. After this time of remembering, the community petitions God to continue his saving works within the Church. We implore him to act now, at this time of Baptism, as he has done throughout history. Like our eucharistic prayer, the calling down of the Holy Spirit, or epiclesis, is the high point of this blessing prayer. The community asks, "May the power of the Holy Spirit, / O Lord, we pray, / come down through your Son / into the fullness of this font, / so that all who have been buried with Christ / by Baptism unto death / may rise again to life with him." [113] The community then declares what it is they want the Holy Spirit to do, which is to raise all those who die with Christ and grant them new life. The prayer ends with a short doxology.

This prayer reminds the assembly of the significance of what happens in the waters of rebirth. It is here that one dies with Christ and rises to new life with Christ. It is here that we become members of Christ's Body and sent forth on mission to share the Good News, and because of this, the community

---

111. Although part of the Celebration of Baptism, the Explanatory Rites are outlined and explained in more detail beginning on page 68.
112. OBC, 279.
113. OBC, 279.

blesses God. The imagery in this text provides rich fodder for reflection and catechesis. Delve into the text when preparing homilies, working with parents during the formation process, and in choosing music.

Options 2 and 3 are written in a call-and-response style with short assembly responses: "Blessed be God," "Hear us, O Lord," or another "suitable acclamation." The ritual text provides an alternate ending for the blessing should the Baptism take place during Easter Time when the water was previously blessed. The alternate ending recognizes that the water has already been consecrated and through this "blessed water" the children may share "in the faith of the Church . . . [and] may have eternal life."[114]

The responsorial nature of these blessings provides a great opportunity to engage the assembly in the prayer. If you choose one of these two options, be sure to print the responses in a worship guide or choose a musical setting of the response that is easy and will help the assembly participate. If the acclamation is to be recited, the priest celebrant should tell the people what the acclamation will be in advance to be sure that they can respond without hesitation. There is no standard ending to each invocation, and so the priest celebrant should indicate the end of each invocation clearly with either a visible gesture or voice inflection.

As you are preparing for this part of the rite, consider what actions or signs might complement the prayer. Depending upon the size and shape of the parish's font, water may be slowly poured into the font during the blessing or the priest celebrant may scoop or stir the water during the prayer. These actions are not prescribed in the rite, but they do allow for the assembly to connect more intimately with the action taking place. These big gestures rouse the sacred imagination. The rite only asks the priest celebrant to touch the water or make the Sign of the Cross over the water after the invocation of the Spirit—this is the visual sign of blessing. The touching and Sign of the Cross are omitted during Easter Time because the water has already been blessed. The goal is not to design a dramatic experience, but simply to highlight the relationship between the prayer and the action. It also visually helps the assembly to participate.

Renunciation of Sin and Profession of Faith

The Renunciation Of Sin and Profession of Faith have been part of the baptismal rite since the earliest centuries of the Church. This is an extremely

---

114. OBC, 223–224.

important part of the rite. "No parent should bring an infant to the waters of baptism without a deep awareness of the ways of evil, even as it enters the life of the family and the very heart of the parent,"[115] and this portion of the rite powerfully reminds parents of the danger of evil.

The Renunciation Of Sin begins with the priest celebrant addressing the parents and godparents directly. There is no option for adapting this address; it should be recited exactly as written. These words are the Church's authoritative admonition to the parents and godparents to impress upon them the seriousness of Baptism. The strong and vivid language reminds them of their responsibility to share the faith and keep the children "reserved from the contagion of sin." It reminds them that they have come here to present these children for baptism; that they are responsible for bringing up their children "in the faith"; and that if their faith makes them "ready to accept this responsibility" they must renew the vows of their own Baptism.[116]

The Renunciation of Sin begins with the priest addressing the parents and godparents directly.

During their formation, parents and godparents should spend considerable time contemplating both this address and the renunciation and profession that follow. The Profession of Faith takes the place of the usual Creed that is said at Mass. They do not make this Profession of Faith for their child but for themselves. This should be an intense part of the rite for the entire assembly. In the early Church when adult Baptism was the norm, the catechumens would face the west, the place of darkness and evil—"the place where Satan dwelt"—and firmly renounce the father of lies.[117] Once Satan was renounced, the catechumen would turn to the east, the place of the rising sun—the place of Christ's light—and make the Profession of Faith. The rite no longer prescribes this action, but this history helps us understand how important and radical it is to give oneself completely over to Christ.

---

115. Gabe Huck, *Infant Baptism in the Parish: Understanding the Rite* (Chicago: Liturgy Training Publications, 1980), p. 45.
116. See OBC, 281.
117. Casimir Kucharek, *The Sacramental Mysteries: A Byzantine Approach* (Allendale, NJ: Alleluia Press, 1976), pp. 105–106, as quoted in Huck, p. 45.

The rite provides two formularies for the Renunciation Of Sin. Both are addressed to both the parents and godparents while the assembly prayerfully listens.[118] Both options consists of three strong questions, and the preparation team might consider asking the parents which formula they prefer after a time of study with these texts. The first option is a longer text but speaks more fully and clearly about sin: "Do you renounce Satan? [I do.] / The author and prince of sin? And all his works? [I do.] / And all his empty show? [I do.] Do you renounce the lure of evil, / so that sin may have no mastery over you? [I do.] / Do you renounce Satan, / the author and prince of sin? [I do.]" The second option is is direct and short: "Do you renounce sin, / so as to live in the freedom of / the children of God? [I do.]"[119] Regardless of the form that is used, the parents and godparents respond together "I do." It may be pastorally advisable to remind parents and godparents of this response prior to the first question.

The second form is followed by a rubric permitting the second form to be "adapted with more precision by the Diocesan Bishop, especially when it is necessary that the parents and godparents should renounce superstitions, divinations, and magical arts practiced with reference to the children."[120] The English-speaking bishops have not created such a form, so one of the two forms that is given should be used as is.

The Profession of Faith follows the Renunciation of Sin. The parents and godparents respond "I do" three times in response to a question-style form of the Apostles' Creed: one for the Father, one for the Son, and one for the Holy Spirit, holy Catholic Church, and so on. The response should make clear that the parents and godparents understand what they are professing and that this part of the rite was explored, prayed with, and embodied during their formation.

At the end of the Profession of Faith, the celebrant says, "This is our faith. This is the faith of the Church. We are proud to profess it in Christ Jesus our Lord."[121] This statement concludes with the assembly's fervent "Amen" and a sign of their assent to the Profession of Faith (recall that *Amen* means "so be it" or "I believe"). The rubric allows for another text or even a song to be sung as the assent, but does not provide a text or even a suggestion. Another way

---

118. See OBC, 121.
119. OBC, 121.
120. OBC, 283.
121. OBC, 284.

to elicit a strong response is for the celebrant to turn physically toward the assembly, raise his voice, or indicate in some other way that they are now being addressed—not just the parents and godparents, as in the prior questions. The celebrant may also chant the formula. Some composers have written music for this profession with assembly responses, such as "Renewal of Baptismal Promises" found in *Who Calls You by Name*, volume I, by David Haas or the Taizé song "There Is One Faith"; this might be viable for your parish.

When preparing this part of the rite, the priest celebrant should consider memorizing the questions that will be used so that he can ask them intentionally, authoritatively, and without hesitation. If the number of children is not too large, the priest celebrant might even consider asking each set of parents and godparents these questions and then immediately baptize that child. This makes an immediate connection to each family. Although this may take a bit more time, it is worth considering and choreographing if chosen.

Further, the parents and godparents must be properly prepared and rehearsed so their response is confident, clear, and loudly spoken such that the Church resounds with their "I do." A server or acolyte holding a microphone may help them to be heard. Ideally, they will have practiced in the baptismal area and feel comfortable speaking loudly. Their fervent witness must be heard within the community.

Baptism

Following the Renunciation Of Sin and Profession of Faith, the priest celebrant invites the first family to approach the font for the celebration of Baptism. The parents present the child to the Church for Baptism, and through the ministers of the Church, Christ baptizes the child. Those preparing the liturgy need to carefully plan where the priest celebrant and other ministers, parents, and godparents will stand. This will depend on the size of and placement of the font. Whatever the positioning, the assembly should be able to see and fully participate. Everyone should rehearse this movement and placement so they are comfortable and familiar with the procedure on the day of the Baptism. This will help the liturgy unfold seamlessly.

The celebrant asks, "Is it your will, therefore, that **N.** should receive Baptism in the faith of the Church, which we have all professed with you?" The parents and godparents reply, "It is." At the time of Baptism, the priest celebrant will ask the parents and godparents to state their intention one final time. Prior to asking the question, it is helpful to indicate who is to answer

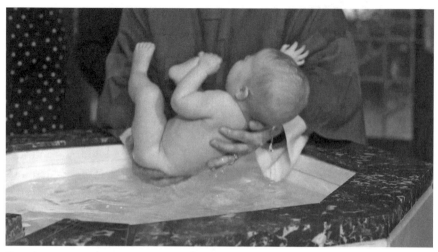
The priest immerses the child in the font three times.

the question (for example, "And so, I ask you, parents and godparents . . ."). By their answer, parents and godparents affirm their commitment to share their faith with the infant.[122]

Then, the priest baptizes each child with a threefold immersion or pouring. Using these exact words, he says "**N., I baptize you in the name of the Father** [he immerses or pours water on the child], / **and of the Son** [he immerses or pours water on the child a second time], / **and of the Holy Spirit** [he immerses or pours water on the child a third time]."[123] This formula comes from Matthew's account of the Gospel when Jesus commands the disciples to go forth and baptize in his name. It has been used since the earliest days of the Church and cannot be changed. Some celebrants use only the first name of the child, while others use the first name and the middle name. This decision should be made based on individual factors, such as whether the child will be referred to by both the first and middle names, or whether the middle name is of particular religious or familial significance.

Prior to the celebration of the liturgy, the parents should discuss whether their child will be immersed or whether the water will be poured upon him or her. Immersion is the preferred method for Baptism because it strongly signifies that the old life has died and was buried with Christ and a new Christian has risen to new life with him. Many people are more familiar with the pouring of water, but by using immersion, the Church invites us to a

---

122. OBC, 285.
123. OBC, 285.

deeper and fuller understanding of the celebration of Baptism. Immersion is the traditional method and has the potential to enrich the community's understanding of the sacrament. It is not a mere rinsing away of sin, but a real encounter with the living God that transforms the child forever.

The way a community celebrates Baptism will speak volumes about how it understands this sacrament. Rather than succumbing to sacramental minimalism, we must ensure that the sacramental rites are celebrated in such a generous and robust way that the symbols convey their meaning and need no further explanation. When the sacrament is celebrated well, it has the potential to catechize the community and form it into a family of disciples. For example, "baptizing infants by full, naked immersion is guaranteed to get an assembly's attention"[124] and really stir their sacramental imagination. Immersion will hopefully inspire the assembly and move them to contemplate what the ritual means in their life and the life of the church.

Common objections to immersion seem to "center on the child's nudity, on the fear of catching cold, or a worry about the baby urinating in the font."[125] Instead of focusing on why immersion will not be successful the community should focus on how to implement it well so it will help the community celebrate the sacrament more fully. Infants have been successfully immersed for more than one thousand five hundred years in the Orthodox Church. The following points will be helpful to refine or begin practicing baptizing by immersion:

- Catechize the community about the Church's preference for immersion. This will not only help them understand the history and theology, but will also reassure them that it is safe for their children.

- Discuss the immersion process with the parents and godparents so they are comfortable with the elements of this part of the rite. It may also be helpful to walk them through the steps at a rehearsal.

- If the font is not heated, a server or catechist can add warm water to the font before the liturgy.[126] If you decide to add water at the blessing of the font, add hot water and the font should be lukewarm by the time the immersion takes place. Be sure to test the water to be sure it is not scalding hot.

---

124. Fitzgerald, p. 51.
125. Huck, p. 49.
126. See CI, 20.

- The priest celebrant should practice baptizing by immersion so that he can confidently, safely, and securely hold a wet child during the rite. In most instances, the infant will enjoy the water.

- The children should be dressed in loose clothing that can be easily removed when they are brought to the church. After the procession to the font, the parents and/or godparents may disrobe the children and wrap them in blankets that they bring to the church. Diapers can be removed immediately after the Renunciation Of Sin and Profession of Faith. Parents may use a towel to wrap their child until his or her turn to be baptized. Then, after the child is baptized, he or she may be wrapped in the same towel. The diapers may be put back on at the same time as the white garments. If a very large number of children are being baptized and it will take some time, diapers may be put back on while the other children are being baptized, ideally at a nearby table or two placed in the area prior to the beginning of the liturgy.

- The priest celebrant holds the infant with both hands and lowers the child into the water three times as the baptismal formula is said so all can hear.

- If the font is not long enough for "dipping," the priest celebrant can sit the baby in the water and hold the child. Then, water is poured over the infant while the baptismal formula is said. Because it is Christ who baptizes through the ministry of the Church, it is the role of the priest celebrant, as head of the parish, to take the child from one of the parent and perform the Baptism. Parents or godparents should not hold the child in place of the priest.

- Once the child has been baptized, the parents or godparents lift the child from the font (or one parent or godparent). The godparents should be ready with a large towel to receive the child from the priest celebrant. The child is diapered as soon as he or she is dry. All the children remain wrapped in a towel until the Explanatory Rites, where the white garment is received.

- Don't worry if accidents happen in the font. Fonts can be cleaned and parents should not be made to feel guilty that their child behaved normally.

If the child is not baptized by immersion, then water is generously poured over the head of the children using either bare hands or, if customary, a shell (a pitcher may also be used). The gesture should be big and generous to signify dying and rising with Christ. A trickle on the forehead cannot effectively communicate this reality. Children may whimper, cry, or scream regardless of the amount of water that is used, so do not skimp on the water. The splashing of water, the sounds from the children, the smiles and laughter of the assembly—these are all part of the ritual moment! This is not the time for minimalism. The preparation team must carefully prepare the rite and the procedures so that the rite flows smoothly and is comfortable for everyone involved.

After each child is baptized and comes up from the font, the assembly, led by the musicians, may sing an acclamation. The acclamation is one of thanksgiving and praise, and singing here expresses the joy of the community. The rite suggests, "Blessed be God, who chose you in Christ" (and alternate options are provided in chapter VII) but any setting of an "Alleluia" is also most appropriate, especially during Easter Time.[127] Whether an Alleluia or another text is used, echoed call-and-response settings work best.

The rubrics are very clear that if there is more than one child, the priest celebrant "asks the same question and does the same for each child to be baptized"[128] as many times as necessary. Here are a few other details to pay attention to during the preparation process:

- If the Baptism is celebrated by the pouring of water, the children should be held by the mother or father. Before the rite was revised in 1969, godparents presented the child and held the child at Baptism. If it remains a custom, a godparent may hold the child.
- The parish should provide large towels for each set of parents. These towels should be reserved for use at infant Baptisms. These too should be placed on a side table near the font for easy access. One of the baptismal preparation volunteers can provide the towel for the godparent to wrap around the child at the appropriate time.
- If the font is big enough, the priest celebrant may choose to step into the font to baptize. If this is the case, be sure you have towels for the floor, for him to dry off after, and proper vesture for use in the water. He can remove his chasuble, but needs to wear a stole while in the water. One of the baptismal preparation volunteers can assist the priest.
- Baptismal candles should be provided as well. Be sure they are taken out of the boxes before the liturgy begins.

---

127. See OBC, 285.
128. OBC, 285.

If the children being baptized do not need to be held (for example, they are old enough to stand), then your preparation team will need to consider how best to celebrate the actual Baptism. The children may be able to walk or kneel in a font for Baptism by immersion. In that case, if they are toddlers or older, they will most likely wear loose garments instead of being baptized without clothes. This can be a simple alb-like garment (not white) that slips over the head and has wide sleeves. Toddlers or older children may wear a T-shirt, swimming trunks, or a bathing suit underneath, which will help the rite be celebrated prudently. After Baptism, the children will change into formal clothes and then be dressed in the white alb (similar to what is done with adult catechumens). If Baptism is being celebrated by pouring, the children may need steps near the font in order to reach to place his or her head over it. These decisions will be affected by the age of the children being baptized and their ability to participate fully, and they should be discussed with parents prior to the Baptism. As necessary, there may need to be a walk-through in advance to prepare the children for the Baptism.

Explanatory Rites

Outline of the Rite
- Anointing after Baptism
- Clothing with a white garment
- Handing on of a lighted candle
- [*Ephphatha*]

Whether Baptism occurred by immersion or by pouring water over the child's head, the Explanatory Rites follow the water bath. Each of these rites are short, but neither the visual symbols nor the spoken words should be rushed or dramatized. Celebrating the rites well is itself catechetical; it explains what the Church means by baptizing new disciples. Items needed for this part of the ritual include the oil of sacred chrism (which should be displayed in a worthy vessel near the font), the white garment for each child, and the baptismal candle.

Anointing after Baptism
From the text provided in the rite, it is clear that this anointing is different from the Anointing before Baptism and the anointing with chrism at the time of Confirmation. This anointing has been part of the Order of Baptism since

at least the second century. It signifies that God has incorporated the child into the household of God. Through the anointing with sacred chrism, the child is conformed to the Anointed One, Christ, and becomes God's vessel.

> Furthermore, to bring to completion the reality of the Sacrament, children should afterwards be formed in the faith in which they have been baptized. The foundation of this formation will be the Sacrament itself which they have already received. Christian formation, which by right is owed to the children, has no other purpose than to lead them little by little to discern God's plan in Christ, so that ultimately they may be able to ratify the faith in which they have been baptized.[129]

The celebrant offers a short, powerful prayer that is said only once regardless of how many children are present. Although only two sentences, the prayer should be said as written without adaptation. It offers a succinct and powerful summation of what has just happened (the Baptism) and what is about to happen (the anointing):

> Almighty God, the Father of our Lord Jesus Christ,
> has freed you from sin,
> given you new birth by water and the Holy Spirit,
> and joined you to his people.
> He now anoints you with the Chrism of salvation,
> so that you may remain members of Christ, Priest, Prophet, and King,
> unto eternal life.
> Amen.[130]

All respond to this prayer with "Amen." Since the prayer does not end "for ever and ever," the celebrant should do his best to indicate the ending of the prayer through cadence and voice inflection, and should be prepared to lead the "Amen."

Unlike Confirmation, when the children will be anointed on the forehead, during the baptismal rite the child is anointed on the crown of the head to signify his or her sharing in Christ's priestly, prophetic, and kingly ministry. The baptized belong to the royal household of God. This anointing should be lavish to help the assembly contemplate God's abundance and remind us that all the baptized belong to God. A dab of oil is not sufficient. The priest celebrant might consider pouring the oil and then carefully rubbing it in.

---

129. OBC, 3.
130. OBC, 287.

The child is clothed with a white garment that has been brought by the family.

The scent of sacred chrism should waft through the baptismal area and capture the attention of those gathered.

The parents should be instructed to allow the oil to soak in and relish the scent that draws our hearts and minds to the Risen Christ. Obviously, if the oil is dripping into the children's eyes, it should be wiped away. Otherwise, this is a moment that can be used in the time of mystagogy with the parents, godparents, and even the assembly. What did you smell? What does the smell remind you of? How have you been called to be a member of God's household?

Clothing with a White Garment

Up to this point, if the children were baptized by immersion, the children remain wrapped in towels for warmth and may have been diapered. The children have come from the waters of rebirth and are now clothed with Christ himself. Before going into the water, the old self was taken off, and Christ's love and mercy has now become the children's way of life. Being made in the image and likeness of God, the children are filled with the dignity bestowed upon them by God. The white garment is a symbol of this new life and dignity. It reminds us of our call to live a holy life united with Christ.

The formula is the same regardless of how many children are being baptized. The priest celebrant begins by saying the names of the children or "(N. and N.)," then continues: "you have become a new creation / and have clothed yourselves in Christ. / May this white garment be a sign to you of your Christian dignity. / With your family and friends to help you by word and example, / bring it unstained into eternal life."[131] As in the postbaptismal anointing, the priest celebrant should inflect the ending of the prayer and be prepared to lead the "Amen" in the absence of a clear cue. Immediately after the prayer, the priest celebrant may add a brief invitation to put on the garment.

As mentioned earlier, in order for the symbol to be effectively communicated to those gathered, the children could be naked for Baptism and then clothed with a white garment that has been brought by the family.[132] In some places, this garment is handed down from generation to generation or the godparents provide the garment. In either case, it is best if the parish does not provide a garment. Once the text for this part of the rite is read, the parents and/or godparents clothe the children with the white garment. This speaks powerfully to the assembly when the child was not already clothed in the baptismal garment for the Baptism. Since many families will be dressing their children, the preparation team may have a changing table available near the font. A simple wooden table, crafted to match the other furniture, with a changing pad is sufficient.

Prior to (and, if absolutely necessary, during the Baptism), the children could be clothed in a simple, solid-colored (not white) onesie or side-tie shirt on top of a swim diaper, with easily removable stretchy pants. After the Baptism and prior to the anointing, the children could be dried with a towel, diapered, then wrapped in a towel until this part of the rite, when the white baptismal garment can be put on over the top of the diaper. Ideally, the white garment will be of such a simple nature that putting it on does not require use of a separate room, either for modesty or time purposes.

If the children are baptized while clothed, this part of the ritual loses the ability to communicate what Baptism has accomplished in the children. Usually, in this scenario, the parish provides a bib-like garment or infant "stole" that is draped over the children, who are already wearing a white garment. This is ritually nonsensical and should be avoided. If the children are already wearing a white garment, there is no need to duplicate symbols, especially with a paper-like bib that lacks continuity with tradition and certainly does not speak to being clothed with the Risen Christ. Paul Turner says that

---

131. OBC, 288.
132. See OBC, 288.

"at worst [this placing of the bib] pretends that the beautiful garment the child is wearing has nothing to do with baptism at all."[133]

Handing On of a Lighted Candle

The *Rite of Christian Initiation of Adults* clearly states what the presentation of the candle means: "The presentation of a lighted candle shows that they are called to walk as befits the children of light."[134] The sharing of this candle helps us understand that in Baptism, each child is filled with the light of Christ and called to go into the world sharing the joy of this light. The newly baptized have been changed, as have the gathered assembly, and therefore, the baptized have a responsibility to "walk always as children of the light."[135]

Once the children are clothed, the priest celebrant "takes the paschal candle and says: 'Receive the light of Christ.'" The rubric says that "One member of each family (e.g., the father or godfather) lights a candle for each child."[136] Practically, this can be tricky. The candle may be too big to move or hold, or it may be awkward trying to hold the candle while reciting the text and getting another candle lit. If the priest celebrant holds the candle, then a server must be present to hold the ritual book. The other servers or a deacon must assist in getting the Paschal candle from its stand into the hands of the minister.

If this becomes too cumbersome, the preparation team might consider having a deacon or server hold the candle while the priest celebrant recites the text and the families come forward to light their candle. If the candle is particularly tall or heavy and cannot be removed easily from its stand, another option is to place a small stool or steps in front of the Paschal candle to make it easy for the person to reach the flame.

If the number of children is not too large, a more intimate adaptation might be to have the priest celebrant hold the Paschal candle and approach each family, of which one person is holding the child's candle. The priest celebrant then says to the person holding the candle, "Receive the light of Christ"[137] and this person lights the child's candle from the flame of the Paschal candle. The priest celebrant then moves to the next family and repeats the process. After all the candles are lit, the priest returns to his place near

---

133. Turner, p. 27.
134. RCIA, 214.
135. OBC, 289; see also John 1:4–5; 1 Thessalonians 5:5; and 1 John 2:9.
136. OBC, 289.
137. OBC, 289.

the font and completes the text that instructs the parents and godparents to keep the candle burning brightly.

Often, parishes buy candles in bulk from catalogues or religious goods stores. These candles are often small, slender, and tend to burn rapidly. Consider purchasing more substantial baptismal candles that are large enough to display in the child's room but not so large that they cannot be easily carried. Baptismal candles can be used in family prayer services around birthdays, feast days, and to mark major events in the child's life. If that is the case, then you need a sizable and beautiful candle. Companies like Marklin Candle Design, Cathedral Candle Company, and Root offer several options and some may even allow you to design a candle that includes the parish logo, name, and the name of the child's patron saint. This is an area to be creative, but not garish, so that the symbol speaks loudly and beautifully. At the time for First Communion and even Confirmation, the parish can request these candles come out of the closet for prayer services and to make strong connections to Baptism. Remember that Baptism and Confirmation depute us to celebrate the Eucharist.

Ephphatha

The word *ephphatha* (ef'-a-tha) is an Aramaic word found in Mark's account of the Gospel, in which Jesus cures the deaf man.[138] It means "be opened." This rite is optional in the United States; however, rather than choosing to omit this rite to save time, the parish preparation team, along with the parents and godparents, should discuss its significance and why it may or may not be important or appropriate to include. In the initiation rites for adults, this rite is celebrated normally with the elect on Holy Saturday during the Preparation Rites.[139]

Like the deaf man whom Jesus cures, the prayer asks that the child's ears be opened to hear the Word proclaimed and the tongue be freed to proclaim the Good News. As the priest celebrant offers the prayer, he touches the ears and the mouth of each child. If there is a large number of children, then he says the prayer once. Celebrating this simple rite can profoundly remind the community that hearing the Word should rouse them to go forth and share their faith in Christ.

---

138. See Mark 7:31–37.
139. See RCIA, 197–199.

Liturgy of the Eucharist

Outline of the Rite

- Preparation of the Gifts
- Prayer over the Offerings
- Preface Dialogue
- Preface
- Preface Acclamation (Holy)
- Eucharistic Prayer
    - Mystery of Faith
    - Doxology/Amen
- The Communion Rite
    - The Lord's Prayer
    - Sign of Peace
    - Lamb of God
    - Invitation to Holy Communion
    - Communion
    - Prayer after Communion

After the Explanatory Rites, the Mass resumes as usual with the Preparation of the Gifts. If the assembly has gathered at the font, the preparation team might consider including a song that can accompany the people's movement to their pews and the Presentation of the Gifts. The song may be baptismal in nature, but it need not be if there has been baptismal music throughout the celebration of the rite. Once everyone is in place and the altar has been prepared, the gifts are presented. One option is to have the families process to their seats in pairs during the Presentation of the Gifts. They can precede the gift bearers and the gifts may be presented by a set of parents and/or godparents. However, ideally the gifts are presented by other ministers (perhaps a family member) or parishioners who can take on this role so that the parents are not unecessarily burdened and the community continues to minister to them. Once the gifts are presented and prepared, the Liturgy of the Eucharist continues in the customary manner as Sunday Mass.

Priest celebrants should be aware that if the ritual Mass, "For the Conferral of Baptism," is prayed, *The Roman Missal* provides special inserts to be used with the four Eucharistic Prayers.[140] For ease, the liturgist or priest may want to write the insert onto a notecard and affix this card into the Missal at the appropriate place in the Eucharistic Prayer that will be prayed during Mass. This not only reminds the priest celebrant of the insert, but allows for a smooth praying of the Eucharistic Prayer because he will not need to turn and flip pages in the Missal. When celebrating the ritual Mass for Baptism, Preface II of Easter may be used during Easter Time. Throughout the rest of the year, Preface I of the Sundays in Ordinary Time may be used.

Communion Rite

The Lord's Prayer is prayed by the assembly in its usual place. After the community shares the Sign of Peace and sings the Lamb of God, the priest celebrant invites the community to the Lord's table with the words, "Behold the Lamb of God, / behold him who takes away the sins of the world. / Blessed are those called to the supper of the Lamb."[141] Immediately after the invitation to Holy Communion, the Communion song begins.[142] The music that accompanies the Communion procession can have a profound impact on those who journey to the Lord's table. It can draw them into the sacred act and therefore make them more aware of Christ's presence and their sharing in his Paschal mystery. Since it accompanies the procession, the music needs to be accessible for the community. This could be a short refrain sung by the assembly with verses sung by a cantor or choir. The text could connect to the Scripture readings and highlight what was celebrated in the baptismal rite earlier (for example, a setting of Psalm 34 or James Chepponis' "As the Bread of Life Is Broken"). Be intentional and discerning when choosing what will help your community enter fully into the act of and responsibility connected with receiving Holy Communion.

As noted in the *Rite of Christian Initiation of Adults*, "it is most desirable that [all] receive communion under both kinds."[143] Although this is not explicitly stated in the *Order of Baptism of Children*, this instruction provides solid guidance, especially for parents and godparents. The *General Instruction of the Roman Missal* is very clear about this expectation: "Holy Communion has a fuller form as a sign when it takes place under both kinds."[144] This best

---

140. The texts for these inserts are found in the ritual Mass itself and not in the section with the Eucharistic Prayers.
141. Order of Mass, 132.
142. See Order of Mass, 136, and GIRM, 86.
143. RCIA, 243; see also GIRM, 281.
144. GIRM, 281.

practice clearly expresses the fullness of the Divine Banquet of which we partake at every Mass and which we will fully celebrate with Christ on that final day in God's Kingdom. Sharing in the Cup of Salvation is a sign of our commitment to Christ and his gift of joy that fills us. As with all banquets, it is a joyful celebration!

It is important for sacristans, liturgists, and ordained ministers to ensure that enough hosts and wine are prepared for the distribution of Communion: "care should be taken to enable the faithful to communicate with hosts consecrated during that Mass."[145] This helps connect the image of the banquet and the fuller sharing in the mystery of Christ. Therefore, retrieving hosts from the tabernacle should only be done if and when hosts run out. By taking hosts from the tabernacle during the Fraction Rite or the Lamb of God, it communicates a disconnect between the liturgical act of communal Eucharistic praying and the act of receiving Communion. The community gathered and prayed the Eucharistic Prayer during this liturgy, and therefore they should receive Communion confected during this liturgy. If extraordinary ministers are needed for the distribution of Holy Communion, the preparation team might consider asking those who are involved with the overall process of baptismal preparation to assist with this ministry. The extraordinary ministers can also be those who are in the normal ministry rotation in the parish, especially since it is the whole parish who celebrated this sacrament with the families. Extraordinary ministers are only needed if there are not enough priests or deacons available, and they must be properly prepared for this ministry.[146]

Care should be taken that both species are offered to the parents, family, and assembly.

As the Communion procession forms, presumably the families who celebrated Baptism are seated near the front of the church. In order to signify the unity of the gathered assembly, these families join the usual procession

---

145. *Eucharisticum mysterium* (EM), 31. See also EM, 32 and 49; BLS, 70; *Gathered in Steadfast Faith*, 28 and 58; CSL, 55; GIRM, 85, 157, 160, 243, 283; *Redemptionis sacramentum* (RS), 89.

146. See *Norms for the Distribution of Holy Communion under Both Kinds in the Dioceses of the United Sates of America*, 28 and 30.

instead of being called one by one and singled out in some way before the others in the assembly are invited forward.

After receiving Holy Communion, the families return to their pew to join in the congregational song and then, when distribution is finished, a time of silent prayer and thanksgiving. A communal song may also be sung after the entire assembly has received Communion. The Communion Rite concludes with the Prayer after Communion.

Concluding Rites

Outline of the Rite

- ["Brief" announcements]
- Blessing and Dismissal
- [Closing song]
- [Dedication of children to the Blessed Virgin]

In the Roman Rite, the Concluding Rites are designed to be brief and simple. After having received the Eucharist, the Church sends the people of God out into the world to share the Good News of salvation. The Concluding Rite includes a blessing and a dismissal. In a sense, there is an urgency in the brevity of this rite. The assembly, now filled with the fire of God's love, is encouraged and inspired to be bread broken for a world in need of healing. From this point forward, the community, week after week, models the Christian life to the newly baptized and helps them understand and live out their commitment to be missionary disciples.

Brief annoucements may be made following the Prayer after Communion.[147] It is important that announcements at this time be succinct so the movement of the rite does not collapse or become unnecessarily prolonged. Because this is a festive day for the whole parish, the preparation team or ministers of hospitality might host a parish social so families and friends can mingle with others in the parish who may wish to share their support, prayer, and congratulations. This invitation can be made at this time.

Following any announcements, the *Order of Baptism of Children* provides four options for the solemn blessing and dismissal at the end of Mass. These blessings are not found in *The Roman Missal*. The first form is a tripartite blessing: one for the mother, one for the father, and one for all who

---

147. See Order of Mass, 140.

are gathered. This form is found in the baptismal ritual text for the celebration of Mass. The second form is another tripartite blessing: one for the newly baptized children, one for the parents, and one for all who are gathered. The third form is a shorter version of the first form. The fourth form is the shortest of all: only a blessing for all who are gathered. Forms 2 through 4 are found in chapter VII of the rite.

Although no closing song is mentioned in the Order of Baptism, it is the custom in the United States for a closing song to be sung at Mass. The families may be invited to remain in their places or to join this final procession (they may follow the liturgical ministers and precede the clergy). Most likely, families will want to gather near the sanctuary or baptismal font for pictures. By joining the procession, it might encourage them to gather at a reception to greet others before taking pictures. This is a time for the community to overflow with hospitality and welcome. If there is a custom of bringing the newly baptized child to a side Marian altar for a prayer of dedication, that may also be done after the liturgy.

Role of the Deacon at Baptisms during Mass

Deacons and their wives often serve as formation leaders and through their own parish ministry may have developed close relationships with couples who wish to have the deacon baptize their children. As noted earlier, bishops, priests, and deacons are the ordinary ministers of Baptism.[148] The *Order of Baptism of Children* does not clarify the role of the deacon at Mass.

In addressing this very question, the United States Bishops' Committee on Divine Worship stated in a recent newsletter:

> The rite says little about the role of deacons in this situation, so it would seem that general liturgical principles provide an answer to this question. Perhaps most importantly, although there is no doubt concerning the validity of Baptisms performed by deacons at Mass (with the priest celebrant standing by as an observer), the traditional role of the deacon is to assist the priest at the liturgy, and not to preside over other sacraments when a priest is celebrating the Mass. As for the other aspects of the celebration, common sense must prevail and there will naturally be circumstances when a deacon may be called upon to take a more active role in the Baptism of children within Mass, for example, when the priest is elderly or if there is a large number of children.

---

148. See CI, 11.

At a Mass in which Baptism takes place, the deacon would, first and foremost, perform his usual roles at Mass: 1) carry the Book of the Gospels in the entrance procession and reverence the altar with the priest; 2) proclaim the Gospel; 3) retain the possibility of preaching the homily (in which case he follows the instructions given in the Order of Baptism, basing his homily on the sacred text but also considering the Baptism being celebrated); 4) read the intercessions in the Prayer of the Faithful, drawn from the Order of Baptism and supplemented with petitions for the needs of the Church and the world; and 5) take on his usual roles in the Liturgy of the Eucharist and Concluding Rites. (In the Universal Prayer at a Baptism within Mass, the deacon reads the petitions, but the priest celebrant leads the invocation of the saints, as indicated by the rubrics.)[149]

Order of Baptism for Several Children

The *Order of Baptism of Children* presumes and, indeed, emphasizes the importance of the Church community in the sacrament. When celebrating the Baptism of children outside of Mass, the Church does prefer that several children be baptized within the same liturgy. Doing so brings together several families thereby creating a truly communal celebration. Such a gathering emphasizes and points to "the faith in which the children are being baptized is a treasure not belonging to the family alone, but to the whole Church of Christ."[150] The rite for this purpose, the Order of Baptism for Several Children, is found in chapter I of the ritual text.

When celebrated without Mass, care must be taken to avoid Baptism perceived as a private family event—as though it were simply a case of one family meeting the priest or deacon in an empty church. To avoid this perception, parish ministers (hospitality minister, musicians, readers, a server, a sacristan) should be present whenever possible. Baptisms may also be scheduled to follow Mass, thereby increasing the likelihood that parishioners will see, hear, and be able to greet the family. Scheduling Baptism immediately after Mass also increases the likelihood

> Liturgical services are not private functions, but are celebrations belonging to the Church, which is the "sacrament of unity," namely, the holy people united. . . .
> —*Constitution on the Sacred Liturgy*, 26

---

149. Newsletter, Committee on Divine Worship; volume LV, May 2019.
150. OBC, 4.

that parish ministers will be present, and it maintains a connection between the celebration of Baptism and the celebration of the Eucharist.

Baptism celebrated without Mass is still liturgy. The baptismal liturgy's source, inspiration, and the model for how it is to be celebrated is the Eucharistic liturgy, with the Church gathered as one. In this sense, Baptism is similar to the Marriage rite. Even when celebrated without Mass, Marriage is still usually celebrated to its fullest ritual potential: a procession, a full Liturgy of the Word, and music—all shared with a community of family members, friends, and others who have joyfully gathered to celebrate the sacrament. So too should Baptism outside of Mass be celebrated in the fullest possible way. All who gather—family, friends, liturgical ministers—should be present for the duration of the celebration.

Regarding the baptismal rites themselves, much of what has been said about Baptism during Mass is applicable without Mass. However, there are a few additional considerations. For Baptisms without Mass, it is wise to have several parishioners present to assist family, friends, and other guests. This role could be filled by those who are responsible for leading baptismal preparation or by parish hospitality ministers. Ideally, these parishioners will be there to greet parents and families, and to distribute worship aids or hymnals, and to answer questions. The presence of these hospitality ministers frees the other ministers to attend to their various roles:

- The sacristans and servers can ensure that all the necessary items (for example, candles, holy oils, towels) have been prepared.

- The readers can review their readings in the ritual books or binders from which they will read. (Using ritual books or binders is preferable to reading from loose sheets of paper, as books and binders are strong visual symbols befitting the Word of God.) Prior to the start of the rite, the books and binders should be in place. The Lectionary or binders should be at the ambo (or wherever the readings will occur). If the *Book of the Gospels* will be carried in procession, it should be in an accessible location.

- The music ministers can prepare their materials and, when appropriate, provide prelude and postlude music. Soft yet buoyant instrumental music is most suitable, as it underscores the joyful nature of the celebration and helps to "assist the gathering assembly in preparing for worship."[151]

---

151. STL, 91.

- The celebrating priest or deacon can prepare his ritual book or binder, and he can vest appropriately in "alb or surplice and stole, and even a cope, in a festive color"[152] Although no color is specified, white or gold vestments are highly appropriate.
- Hospitality ministers should prepare the assembly prior to the start of the liturgy.

Outline of the Rite
- Rite of Receiving the Children
    - [Song]
    - Gathering at doors of the church [or other place in church]
    - Address to the parents and godparents
    - Questioning of the parents and godparents
    - Signing of the children's forehead with the cross
    - Procession to the appointed place/song
- Sacred Celebration of the Word of God
    - Biblical readings [one or more[153]]
    - Homily
    - Prayer of the Faithful and Litany of Saints
    - Prayer of Exorcism and Anointing before Baptism
    - [Procession to the font]
- Celebration of Baptism
    - Blessing and invocation of God over the water
    - Renunciation of Sin and Profession of Faith
    - Baptism by immersion or pouring
    - [Acclamation]
- Explanatory Rites
    - Anointing after Baptism
    - Clothing with a white garment
    - Handing on of a lighted candle
    - *Ephphatha*

---
152. OBC, 35.
153. If there is more than one reading, add the singing of a Responsorial Psalm. If a Gospel is proclaimed, include a sung Gospel acclamation.

- Conclusion of the Rite
  - Lord's Prayer
  - Blessing and Dismissal
  - [Closing song]
  - [Dedication of the children to Mary]

Rite of Receiving the Children

The rite begins with the reception of the children. Prior to the arrival of the presiding minister (the rite may be presided over by a priest or deacon) and any other ministers (servers, readers, and so on), "the faithful sing a suitable Psalm or hymn, if circumstances allow."[154] Any of the various acclamations and hymns listed in the rite are appropriate, so choose one based on what is familiar to your community. It takes place just as it does at Mass, ideally beginning at the entrance of the church. Those who have not gathered at the doors of the church should be invited to stand and face the doors so to participate in the Rite of Reception. Unlike at Mass, there is no formal Sign of the Cross or greeting; instead, the welcoming of the child is the focus of this rite. The text is provided in the ritual text. After the presider greets and addresses those who have gathered, "especially the parents and godparents,"[155] the parents are asked to state the name of their child and what they ask of the Church for their child. The presider then addresses and questions the parents and godparents about their readiness and willingness to raise this child in the faith. Then the presiding minister traces the cross on the children's forehead.

After the children are signed with the cross, the presiding minister invites all present to "take part in the celebration of the Word of God."[156] This enables a procession to take place from the entrance of the church to where the readings will be proclaimed (either in the church or in the baptistry). This procession is beneficial during Baptism without Mass, as it enables the readings to be read from the ambo. As for the song, it is usually most effective when parish musicians lead the singing of a simple song with a refrain that can be sung while processing, either a cappella or accompanied. The procession should at least be led by a server carrying the cross (or, if there is no

---

154. OBC, 35.
155. OBC, 36.
156. OBC, 42.

server, by a hospitality minister). Hospitality ministers should follow so that they can direct families to the proper place. The families are then followed by readers and the presiding minister. Unlike at Mass, there is no Gloria or Collect. Instead, once all have reached their seats, they may be seated for the Liturgy of the Word. As discussed earlier, there is an option for children to be carried to a separate place during the Liturgy of the Word, but generally the children should remain with their families.[157]

> The many riches contained in the one word of God are admirably brought out in the different kinds of liturgical celebration and in the different gatherings of the faithful who take part in those celebrations.
>
> —Introduction to the *Lectionary for Mass*, 3

Liturgy of the Word

For Baptisms without Mass, there are no prescribed readings for the day, so the readings can be chosen and the homily tailored specifically for the baptismal rite. The rite provides flexibility with how many readings are chosen when taking place without Mass. One or two passages may be read with an optional Responsorial Psalm or acclamation sung between them. Parish preparation teams, the presiding minister, and the parents may consider numerous factors when selecting the readings. Perhaps there is a specific allusion to Scripture in the liturgical environment (on the font, in the baptistry, or in the church). Perhaps there is a reading that is well suited for the liturgical season. If only one child is being baptized, perhaps there is a reading that is of special significance for the family.

There is no need for the presiding minister to offer additional commentary or announcements before each reading is read (for example: "And now we will hear **N.** read the First Reading, taken from the Old Testament . . ."). Rather, those who proclaim the readings should proceed with the same wording and dialogues that are used during Mass (that is, "A reading from the book . . ." / "The Word of the Lord"). The presiding minister should always proclaim the Gospel reading, but when two readings are used, a reader (friend or family member or parish reader) may proclaim the First Reading from the Old Testament or New Testament.

Parish communities should make every effort to provide music ministers for baptismal liturgies taking place outside of Mass. It is the preferred practice

---

157. See OBC, 43.

that the Responsorial Psalm be sung. Parish cantors should be present to lead the Responsorial Psalm, the Gospel acclamation, and the Litany of Saints. There is also an option for a suitable song or a period of silence after the homily.[158] A song is most appropriate when parish musicians are present to lead it.

The rite specifies that during the Liturgy of the Word, "all are seated."[159] If a procession has occurred and people are seated in the pews, then it makes ritual sense to follow the same postures as during Mass: to be seated for the First Reading and Responsorial Psalm (and Second Reading, if there is one), to stand for the Gospel (a Gospel procession may occur), and to be seated for the homily. If one reading is being proclaimed it makes sense to remain standing. Silence may follow the readings, psalm, and homily. After the homily, the rite also provides the option for an optional song. The preparation team should look at these options for inspiration, then consider which ones are familiar to the community.

The Prayer of the Faithful follows the homily (period of silence/song). Parishes may use what is included in the rite, the alternative texts in the appendix, or write their own prayers.[160] The *Order of Baptism* specifies that the petitions are read by a lector (or reader). While they can certainly be read by the presiding minister, this is a fitting moment for the involvement of those persons who have led baptismal preparation sessions for the families of the children being baptized. The presence of such a minister further strengthens the link to the Church community as a whole, especially for Baptisms without Mass. The Litany of Saints, Prayer of Exorcism, and the Anointing before Baptism follow just as they do at Mass.[161]

At this point, if the Liturgy of the Word has taken place away from the font, there is a procession to the font for the Baptism. As discussed earlier, the instructions in the rite are thorough:[162] if the baptistry is outside the church or not within view of the congregation, all process there. If the baptistry is within view, only the celebrant, parents, and godparents go there with the children. If the baptistry cannot accommodate the congregation, the Baptism is celebrated "in a more suitable place."[163] A temporary font might need to be used in order to accommodate the congregation if every family is

---

158. See OBC, 46.
159. OBC, 44.
160. See OBC, 47, 217–220.
161. See page 49.
162. See OBC, 52; see also page 54.
163. OBC, 52.

unable to gather around the font at the same time. It is never a good practice to leave families in the church to wait until it is their turn for their child to be baptized.

Psalm 23 or another song may be sung during the procession to the font "if it can be done with dignity."[164] For Baptisms without Mass, the amount of time that the procession will take, the presence or absence of parish musicians, and the familiarity of an appropriate psalm setting are all factors to consider when deciding what to sing.

Celebration of Baptism and the Explanatory Rites

The celebration of the sacrament—that is, the blessing of water, Renunciation of Sin, Profession of Faith, Baptism, and the explanatory rites (anointing with chrism, clothing with white garment, and presentation of the lighted candle)—are celebrated just as they would be at Mass.[165] Parish teams should make every effort to incorporate the singing of an acclamation immediately after each child is baptized, even without Mass.[166] As mentioned earlier, a call-and-response acclamation is usually most effective, whether it is one of the suggested acclamations in the rite, chapter VII, or a simple, joyful "Alleluia."

Conclusion of the Rite

If the font is located in a place apart from the altar, a procession to the altar takes place for the praying of the Lord's Prayer. The procession happens after the *ephphatha,* or, if this prayer was omitted, the lighting of the baptismal candles. It is important to make use of this procession. Processing to the altar embodies the very movement that the baptismal rite anticipates in the life of the newly baptized—the journey toward the completion of initiation with the reception of the Eucharist. Explicitly mentioning that connection makes the procession more meaningful, particularly when Baptism is celebrated without Mass.

The rite provides guidance for the procession. First, "the lighted candles of the newly baptize are carried."[167] The presiding minister should articulate this to the parents and godparents as he gives directions for the procession; otherwise, those who are holding the candles may be uncertain about whether

---

164. OBC, 52.
165. Refer to page 68.
166. See OBC, 60.
167. OBC, 67.

or not to extinguish them. Second, a song may be sung, either "Baptized in Christ, / you are clothed with Christ, / alleluia, alleluia" or one of the other acclamations provided in chapter VII of the rite.[168] If a short acclamation is sung, responsorial or call-and-response settings are most effective. The order of the procession should follow the same order as the earlier procession (between the reception of the children and the Liturgy of the Word).

The praying of the Lord's Prayer takes place in the sanctuary.

After the procession has concluded, all say or sing the Lord's Prayer. The introduction to the Lord's Prayer looks forward to the time when the newly baptized will receive the other sacraments of Christian initiation: Confirmation and Holy Communion.[169] The wording of the introduction may be adapted. If the prayer is to be chanted, a fitting introduction would be to recite the first part as it is written in the rite and then to chant the introduction to the Lord's Prayer using the invitation from Mass ("At the Savior's command / and formed by divine teaching, / we dare to say").

After the Lord's Prayer, the rite concludes with the blessing and dismissal. As mentioned earlier, there are four forms of the blessing. The second option is the only option explicitly blessing the newly baptized children. No matter which form of the blessing is chosen, it is followed by the Trinitarian dismissal formula, in which everybody is blessed in the name of the Father, Son, and Holy Spirit. It concludes as Mass does: "Go in peace. Thanks be to God."[170]

After the blessing and dismissal, "if circumstances permit, a suitable canticle that expresses paschal joy and thanksgiving or the Canticle of the Blessed Virgin Mary, the *Magnificat*, may be sung by all."[171] The hymn that is sung should be familiar and joyful. If the rite began with a procession, it is certainly fitting to end with a liturgical procession, led by the crossbearer. Instrumentalists may choose to play a postlude, but if people are remaining

---

168. See OBC, 67, 225–245.
169. See OBC, 68.
170. OBC, 70.
171. OBC, 71.

in place to take photos, simply finishing with the hymn is appropriate. If there is a custom of bringing the newly baptized child to a side Marian altar, that may also be done after the final blessing.

Order of Baptism for One Child

Outline of the Rite
- Rite of Receiving the Child
  - [Song]
  - Gathering at doors of the church [or other place in church]
  - Address to the parents
  - Questioning of the parents and godparents
  - Signing of the child's forehead with the cross
  - Procession to appointed place/song
- Sacred Celebration of the Word of God
  - Biblical readings [one or more[172]]
  - Homily
  - Prayer of the Faithful and Litany of Saints
  - Prayer of Exorcism and Anointing before Baptism
  - [Procession to the font]
- Celebration of Baptism
  - Blessing and invocation of God over the water
  - Renunciation of Sin and Profession of Faith
  - Baptism by immersion or pouring
  - [Acclamation]
- Explanatory Rites
  - Anointing after Baptism
  - Clothing with a white garment
  - Handing on of a lighted candle
  - *Ephphatha*

---

172. If there is more than one reading, add the singing of a Responsorial Psalm. If a Gospel is proclaimed, include a sung Gospel acclamation.

- Conclusion of the Rite
  - Lord's Prayer
  - Blessing and Dismissal
  - [Closing song]
  - [Dedication of the child to Mary]

Chapter II of the *Order of Baptism of Children* includes the Order of Baptism for One Child. As noted earlier, it is the Church's preference to baptize more than one child at the same liturgy. In smaller parishes or parishes that do not have many young families, sometimes there are no opportunities for several infants to be baptized at once. Given the directive that an infant should be baptized within the first weeks of his or her life, celebrating the Order of Baptism for One Child enables a child to be baptized without an unduly long wait. Even in larger parishes where Baptisms are celebrated on a regular schedule, sometimes there is an interval when only one child is born. In those instances, the Order of Baptism for One Child should be used.

Everything that has already been said regarding the careful preparation and celebration of the rite for several children also applies to this rite—even when only one child is baptized. Baptism should still be celebrated joyfully and fully. Processions, music, and other elements of the rite should never be omitted or minimized just because only one child is being baptized. Especially in parishes that do not have many young families, the birth and Baptism of a child is indeed a joyous event for the entire community.

Most of what has been said about the baptismal rite for several children also applies to the rite for one child, but there are a few notable differences. The most notable difference is that throughout the rite for one child, singular language (he/she/him/her/child) is used instead of plural language (they/them/children). Parish prepration teams should also note the following:

- *Celebrating the rite without processions*: As in the other ritual forms, the rite for baptizing a single child presumes a stational liturgy complete with processions. However, if pastoral considerations require that the rite be celebrated in a single location, it should be around the font. An adequate number of sturdy chairs (ideally, non-folding, non-metal) may be placed around the font in advance and a dignified lectern used for the proclamation of the Word. Liturgical ministers (music, readers, hospitality, servers) will still be needed, although family members may be encouraged to participate in this form of the rite, especially as readers. Parish teams will need to work with them in advance so that they can proclaim the readings properly and with dignity.

- *Receiving of the Child*: This portion of the rite is celebrated as it is in the order for several children. There is only one significant omission: the rite for one child does not include a directive suggesting that the child may be taken to a separate place during the Liturgy of the Word. The reasons for this omission are unclear. In any case, as discussed earlier, it is best practice for the child to remain for the Liturgy of the Word.

- *Liturgy of the Word*: The readings, homily, Prayer of the Faithful, Litany of Saints, Prayer of Exorcism, and Anointing before Baptism are celebrated as in the rite for several children. With only one child being baptized, preparation teams, presiding ministers, and parents can take special care to select readings that are suited for the Baptism of this particular child.

- *Procession to the Font*: The only difference between the rite for one child and the rite for several children concerns the procession after the Anointing before Baptism. As discussed earlier, the rite for several children offers various options for those who should process to the bapistry depending on its location and the number of people present. The rite for one child simply presumes that everybody will join the procession; it says, "Then they proceed to the baptistry, or, if circumstances suggest, to the sanctuary, if the Baptism is celebrated there."[173] The rite assumes that with only one child being baptized, there will be a comparatively small number of people present, so processing and gathering around the font will not pose insurmountable difficulties.

- *Celebration of the Sacrament/Explanatory Rites*: All elements of the celebration of the sacrament (the blessing of the water, Renunciation of Sin and Profession of Faith, the Baptism itself) and the Explanatory Rites (anointing with chrism, clothing with white garment, lighted candle, and *ephphatha*) are performed the same as they were in the rite for several children.[174]

- *Conclusion of the Rite*: As in the rite for several children, the rite concludes with a procession, the Lord's Prayer, a final blessing, and an optional hymn. Only one form of the final blessing is provided in the rite itself. The one provided is also option 1 in the rite for several

---

173. OBC, 89.
174. See OBC, 90–101.

Preparing the Order of Baptism of Children

children. However, options 2 through 4 may also be used. These other forms are found in chapter VII of the rite.

Order of Baptism for a Large Number of Children

Outline of the Rite
- Rite of Receiving the Children
  - [Song]
  - Gathering at doors of the church [or other place in church]
  - Address to the parents
  - Questioning of the parents and godparents
  - Signing of the cross over all the children
- Sacred Celebration of the Word of God
  - Biblical readings [one or more[175]]
  - Homily
  - Prayer of the Faithful
  - [Litany of Saints]
  - Prayer of Exorcism
  - Procession to the font
- Celebration of Baptism
  - Blessing and invocation of God over the water
  - Renunciation of Sin and Profession of Faith
  - Baptism by immersion or pouring
  - [Acclamation]
- Explanatory Rites
  - Anointing after Baptism
  - Clothing with white garment
  - Lighted candle
- Conclusion of the Rite
  - Lord's Prayer
  - Blessing and Dismissal
  - [Closing song]

---

175. If there is more than one reading add the singing of a Responsorial Psalm. If a Gospel is proclaimed include a sung Gospel acclamation.

The Order of Baptism found in chapter III is to be used for a large number of children. What constitutes a large number of children? The rite never defines "a large number" or explicitly indicates how to discern when this form of the rite should be used, just as the rite for several children never defines or gives a specific number for "several."

The rite does offer some clues for how to distinguish between "several" and "a large number" of children. As will be discussed below, the rite for a large number of children omits specific elements (for example, the Anointing before Baptism, the Litany of the Saints, some music). The omission of these elements suggests that pastorally, this rite is intended for missionary territories where, because of the lack of priests, the celebration of Mass and the other sacraments is a rare occasion. In those situations, parishes might celebrate the sacraments *en masse;* that is, during a daylong event for the entire community. The number of children being baptized and the number of people gathered would be extraordinarily large. Combined with the possible need to celebrate other sacraments (such as Confirmation, Reconciliation, Anointing of the Sick, Eucharist) on the same day, time limitations would necessitate the omission of some elements in the baptismal rite.

In many parishes in the United States, such a situation is a rare occurrence. Often, then, using the rite for several children is preferable in order to avoid omitting parts of the rite. However, there may be some parishes where the number of children needing to be baptized along with the limitations on clergy may necessitate use of this form of the rite. The preparation team, along with the pastor, will want to discuss what rite will be used by the parish in these cirumstances. If your team desires to use this form for a large number of children, you may want to discuss the situation with the local diocesan worship office.

If you do celebrate this rite, all of the principles outlined earlier for the other forms of Baptism should be employed; it should be celebrated joyfully and prayerfully with parish hospitality ministers, musicians, and other parishioners present. With the large number of people present, special attention should be given to preparing the liturgical environment and coordinating movement from place to place.

Reception of the Children

Unlike the Order of Baptism for One Child and the Order of Baptism for Several Children, this rite does not indicate if the celebration occurs on Sunday or in the midst of the community. It simply begins by saying that "the faithful sing a suitable Psalm"[176] as the celebrant goes to meet the parents, godparents, and children, either at the church entrance or wherever they are waiting.

After the celebrant informally greets all present, the questions to the parents and godparents vary slightly from the other forms. There are two options. In the first option the initial question is "What name do you give (or: have you given) your children?" The question is asked once and then everyone answers in turn. If the number of children is so large that asking names would be prohibitive, the presider may chose the second option, which skips the naming and proceeds immediately to the next question: "Parents and godparents, who are present here with these children, what do you ask of God's Church for them?" The answer is "Baptism," declared in unison. The rubric does not provide alternate responses as in the other forms.[177]

For the tracing of the cross, the celebrant simply makes the Sign of the Cross over the gathered crowd instead of individually on each child's forehead. The parents and godparents are still invited to sign the child's forehead.

Unlike the other forms, there is no directive for a procession to where the Liturgy of the Word will take place. However, if the celebrant has met the families at the entrance to the church, a procession is necessary and it should be a liturgical procession as in the other forms of the rite with a crossbearer leading the way into the church. As in the other forms, Psalm 85 or other appropriate music may be sung.

Sacred Celebration of the Word of God

Although this form of the rite suggests the reading of Matthew 28:18–20, it is certainly permissible to replace this passage with one of the other readings included in the rite.[178] There is no mention of singing a Responsorial Psalm or Gospel acclamation; this could also be done, nonetheless. After the Liturgy of the Word, there is a brief homily, which is followed by the Prayer of the Faithful.[179] However, the Litany of the Saints and the Anointing before Baptism

---

176. OBC, 107.
177. See OBC, 108.
178. See OBC, 112.
179. See OBC, 113–114.

are omitted. After the Prayer of Exorcism, the celebrant does not lay his hand on each child; he simply "lays hands over all the children at once"[180] and says the prescribed prayer. These omissions and modifications are intended to avoid unduly prolonging the rite owing to the large number of children.

After the imposition of hands, the rite indicates that, "they proceed to the place in which the Baptism is celebrated."[181] Presumably, with a large number of children present, "they" is referring to the celebrant, parents, godparents, and children to be baptized—not to the entire congregation. This movement must be carefully choreographed if there is truly a large number gathered.

Celebration of Baptism

For the blessing and invocation of God over baptismal water, a short responsory form is included in the rite. It consists of short proclamations by the celebrant alternating with the congregation speaking or singing "Blessed be God"[182] or another acclamation. The use of a responsory formula allows for the congregation to engage more fully in this portion of the liturgy. The Renunciation of Sin and Profession of Faith follows. It proceeds as in the forms for baptizing several children or one child.

The Baptism itself has a number of noteworthy differences from the other forms. Most notably, when there is a large number of children, the rite permits other ordained ministers to assist with Baptism. If there are several ministers, each of them—not just the primary celebrant—asks each set of parents and godparents, "Is it your will, therefore, that **N.** should receive Baptism in the faith of the Church . . . ?"[183] immediately before baptizing the child.

Even though the rite makes provision for additional ministers, it does not indicate whether more than one font should be used. Presumably, the use of other fonts is permissible; otherwise there would be no reason to have additional ministers baptizing. If several ministers are assisting, provisions must be made to ensure beautiful and proper fonts for the Baptism. If there is one primary font in which the water has been blessed, the additional fonts

---

180. OBC, 115.
181. OBC, 116.
182. OBC, 118.
183. OBC, 124.

should be filled using that blessed water immediately prior to the first child being baptized.

Also, while the Baptisms are being performed, the community can sing hymns, make acclamations, proclaim passages from Scripture, or maintain silence. These options are a significant departure from the rites for several children and one child, when an acclamation was sung as each child came out of the water. With a large number of children being baptized, singing is an excellent way to keep the community engaged. You might consider mixing songs and readings if the Baptisms are particularly lengthy.

Once all of the children have been baptized, the presider says the prayer for the anointing after Baptism one time. Then the ministers who assisted with the Baptism anoint each child on the crown of the head with the sacred chrism. This anointing may be omitted at the discretion of individual bishops' conferences; however, in the United States it may never be omitted. No direction is given for how the chrism should be distributed to the ministers. If necessary, it may be divided into small vessels in advance.

The clothing with the white garment proceeds as in the forms for one child and several children. For the lighting of the baptismal candle, "the head of one family"[184] lights his candle from the Paschal candle and passes the flame on to the other families. In the rite for a large number of children, the *ephphatha* is omitted, so a song is sung as the candles are lit.

The rite indicates that if the Baptisms were performed somewhere other than a sanctuary, there should then be a procession to the altar. No direction is given regarding music for the procession. Depending on the circumstances, the song that was sung as the candles are lit may be continued during the procession or a different song may be sung. If necessary, directions for the procession should be given prior to the lighting of the candles to ensure that all understand how and when to process.

Conclusion of the Rite

The rite concludes with the Lord's Prayer and the final blessing. Only one form of the final blessing is included in the rite itself—a short formula that is similar to (but not exactly the same as) the fourth form from the other rites. The other formulas may also be used if desired.

---

184. OBC, 127.

As in the orders for one child and several children, all may then sing either a hymn that "expresses paschal joy and thanksgiving"[185] or the Magnificat. Unlike the other rites, no mention is made of bringing the baptized children to the altar of the Blessed Virgin Mary.

Order of Baptism of Children to Be Used by Catechists in the Absence of a Priest or Deacon

A catechist is one who is "in communion with the Bishop . . . [and one who] hands on the word in a complete way and witnesses to the reality of the Church."[186] A catechist's ministry is intimately linked with that of the bishop's ministry, especially, to pass on the faith and help rouse the hearts and minds of all believers. The diocesan bishop is the chief catechist and, when called upon by the bishop, properly formed catechists can be entrusted with the pastoral formation of a community and the celebration of some rites with adaptations.[187] It is the bishop's responsibility to ensure that catechists are "prepared to fulfill their function properly."[188] For example, in the *Rite of Christian Initiation of Adults*, a properly trained catechists can be commissioned "to celebrate the minor exorcisms . . . and the blessings of the catechumens."[189]

In mission territories where there are fewer priests and deacons, catechists are extremely important in collaborating with and assisting the bishop in the ministry of formation. Bishops greatly rely on well-formed catechists to serve a faith community by preparing its members to receive the sacraments, to preside over the sacramental rites (when appropriate), and to accompany the members of the faithful as they strive to live out their call to be disciples. In these circumstances, catechists are not untrained volunteers; they are the ones from within a faith community who have been identified and called forth because of the gifts the Spirit has given them and who are adequately trained to perform these ministerial duties.[190] Recognizing this

---

185. OBC, 131.
186. *General Directory for Catechesis*, 219a.
187. See CCL, 228 §1.
188. CCL, 780.
189. RCIA, 12.
190. See CCL, 785 and 843 §2. Keep in mind that the United States is considered mission territory. There are rural areas in this country in which this rite will be used. Refer to this website for more information: www.usccb.org/catholic-giving/opportunities-for-giving/catholic-home-missions-appeal/what-are-home-missions.cfm.

pastoral need, the *Constitution on the Sacred Liturgy* requested that a shorter rite for infant Baptism be created for use in these mission territories: "Moreover, a shorter rite is to be drawn up, especially in mission lands, for use by catechists, but also by the faithful in general, when there is danger of death and neither a priest nor a deacon is available."[191] Chapter IV of the *Order of Baptism of Children* includes this shorter form of the baptismal rite.

The rite provided in chapter IV will look very familiar to the catechist. This form of the baptismal liturgy is structured similarly to that of the Order of Baptism for Several Children or for One Child—slight adaptations were made to accommodate the catechists:

In the shorter Order of Baptism for the use of catechists the rite of reception of the children, the celebration of the Word of God, or the instruction of the minister, and the Prayer of the Faithful, take place. Before the font, the minister offers a prayer invoking God and recalling the history of salvation with respect to Baptism. After the baptismal washing, the anointing with Chrism is omitted and the adapted formula is recited instead. The whole rite is completed with the usual conclusion. Thus the exorcism, the anointing with the Oil of Catechumens, the anointing with Chrism, and the "Ephphatha" are omitted.[192]

> Local ordinaries are to take care that catechists are duly prepared to fulfill their function properly, namely, that continuing formation is made available to them, that they understand the doctrine of the Church appropriately, and that they learn in theory and in practice the methods proper to the teaching disciplines.
>
> —*Code of Canon Law*, 780

Even though a bishop, priest, or deacon is not presiding, this is still a liturgy of the Church, and the same care and conscious effort should be made to prepare these liturgies when a catechist presides. As a public liturgy—a public sacrament—the parish community should be invited to attend. Parish liturgical ministers should be invited to serve, from music ministry to hospitality. Proper liturgical books should be used—that is, the *Lectionary for Mass* and the *Order of Baptism of Children* or elegant ritual binders rather than loose sheets of paper. Ministers (including family members who might be selected to proclaim the ministers) should be trained and prepared.

---

191. CSL, 68.
192. OBC, 20.

Outline of the Rite
- Rite of Receiving the Children
  - [Song]
  - Gathering at doors of the church [or other place in church]
  - Address to the parents and godparents
  - Questioning of the parents and godparents
  - Signing of the children's forehead with the cross
- Sacred Celebration of the Word of God
  - Readings [one or more[193]]
  - Homily or short talk [explanation of the reading]
  - Prayer of the Faithful and Litany of Saints
- Celebration of Baptism
  - Blessing and invocation of God over the water
  - Renunciation of Sin and Profession of Faith
  - Baptism by immersion or pouring
  - [Acclamation/song]
  - Clothing with a white garment
  - Handing on of the lighted candle
- Conclusion of the Rite
  - Lord's Prayer
  - Blessing and Dismissal
  - [Closing song]

Rite of Receving the Children

The liturgy presumes that a community of the faithful has gathered to celebrate this important moment in the life of the child. A familiar baptismal or joyful gathering song may be sung while the catechist and other ministers approach the door of the church or the place where the parents and godparents are waiting. Depending on the space, the parents and godparents may be waiting near the baptismal font, near the ambo, or another suitable space such as a devotional area or shrine in the church. As in the other forms of

---

193. If there is more than one reading add the singing of a Responsorial Psalm. If a Gospel is proclaimed include a sung Gospel acclamation.

the rite, once the song has ended the catechist informally greets those gathered, especially the parents and godparents (there is no Sign of the Cross). Like the other forms of the rite, the address is provided.

The greeting is followed by the questions for the parents and godparents of the children to be baptized and the signing of the cross on each child's forehead. After the Rite of Receiving the Children, the catechist invites those gathered to listen to God's Word in the Scriptures. The rite does not provide guidance for how this transition is to take place; however, here are a few options:

- *Gathered at the Font*: If the whole assembly, including parents and godparents, are gathered around the baptismal font and this is the primary place for the celebration, then the assembly does not need to process to another location for the Liturgy of the Word. Instead, the minister simply invites the assembly to hear God's Word. You might consider providing seats for friends and family around the baptismal font if there is not a large number of people.

- *Gathered at the Entrance of the Church*: If the whole assembly, including parents and godparents, are gathered at the entrance of the church, then the assembly should process to another location to hear the Word of God—this may be to the inside of the church so that the readings are proclaimed from the ambo or to the font itself (if the font is in another location). A song may accompany the procession.

- *Seated Assembly:* If the assembly is seated in pews and the families, along with the ministers, are gathered at the entrance of the church, we turn to tradition to help us. Normally, the liturgical act begins with a procession of the ministers from the entrance of the nave to the sanctuary or place for the ministers. The best and normative practice is to form a procession once the families are greeted and the children received. As the procession moves to the place for the Liturgy of the Word, the community may sing a suitable song that highlights the gift of Baptism, God's invitation to new life, or something similar.

Sacred Celebration of the Word of God

At first glance, this form of the rite gives the impression that only one reading from the Gospel according to Matthew is proclaimed. Catechists and parish preparation teams most certainly have the option to consider a fuller celebration of the Liturgy of the Word. This option is provided in the rubrics themseves.[194] If it seems pastorally prudent, consider minimally including a reading from the Old Testament or epistles, a sung Responsorial Psalm, Gospel acclamation, and a Gospel reading. The rite provides many options for the readings.[195]

Catechists may be permitted by the bishop to deliver "a brief Homily."[196] This may be a previously prepared text from either the bishop or the pastor or, if properly prepared, the catechist. In order to give an instruction, the catechist should be trained in preaching and the Scriptures and be formally deputed by the bishop.[197] This ministry is very important in breaking open the readings as well as the rite, so the catechist must have "a well-trained tongue."[198]

The rite also permits the omission of the Scripture reading(s) and/or the instruction. If this is the case, the catechists can give the talk that is prescribed in the ritual text.[199] This text is a short exposition on Baptism, which can also be used in the formation of parents and godparents before the liturgical celebration.

Following the homily or instruction, a moment of silence may be observed to allow the Scripture and reflection to soak in and wash over the hearts and minds of those gathered. This will allow some space to help the assembly prepare for the Baptism itself. After a brief silence, all stand and continue the celebration with the Universal Prayer. The intercessions conclude with the Litany of the Saints. In this form of the rite, the Prayer of Exorcism and the Anointing before Baptism, which normally follow the Litany of Saints, are omitted.

Celebration of Baptism

In this form of the rite, there is no clear direction that calls for a procession to the font. It simply says they "go to the baptismal font."[200] If the assembly has not yet gathered near the font, they may process to the font immediately

---

194. See OBC, 137.
195. Additional readings are provided in chapter VII of the *Order of Baptism of Children* and in the ritual Masses section in volume IV of the *Lectionary for Mass*.
196. SCAP, 196.
197. See CCL, 230 §3 and 766 as well as the United States bishops' complementary legislation regarding canon 766 found here: www.usccb.org/beliefs-and-teachings/what-we-believe/canon-law/complementary-norms/canon-766-lay-preaching.cfm.
198. Isaiah 50:4.
199. See OBC, 138.
200. OBC, 141.

following the Litany of Saints. The rite indicates that the parents and godparents are carrying the children and the catechist joins them at the font.[201]

Two forms of the blessing of water are provided. The first form is used if the water has not been blessed, and the second form is used if the water has been blessed. The first form is similar to those found in the other forms of the rite, and it is prayed by the catechist who stands at the font with his or her hands joined. The prayer is a series of invocations after which the people respond with "Blessed be God," or some other suitable acclamation.[202] It might be helpful to sing a familiar acclamation such as an Alleluia, so that all can comfortably participate. Unless the assembly knows their response will be "Blessed be God," they may not confidently respond. The second form, as an invocation upon already blessed water, recognizes God the Father as the source of all creation, and that it is through the waters of Baptism that this new child of God will be born again and received into the salvation won by God's only Son.

After the water has been blessed or the invocation said over the previously blessed waters, the catechist asks the parents and godparents to profess their faith by responding to a series of questions. The Renunciation of Sin takes the same form as presented in the other forms of the rite. A suitable song, which expresses the community's faith, may also be used if this is more pastorally effective.[203]

The Baptism of the children follows the Renunciation of Sin. When a catechist baptizes, the same norms apply as they do for an ordained minister: true water, the Trinitarian words, and immersion is the preferred form. When baptizing the child, the catechist immerses or pours water upon the child three times while saying, "**N., I BAPTIZE YOU IN THE NAME OF THE FATHER, AND OF THE SON, AND OF THE HOLY SPIRIT.**" The rite notes that if there are large numbers of children, additional catechists may help with the Baptisms.[204] The rite also notes:

> If the Baptism is celebrated by the pouring of water, it is preferable for the child to be held by the mother (or by the father); however, where it is felt that the existing custom should be retained, the child may be held by the

---

201. See OBC, 141.
202. See OBC, 142.
203. See OBC, 147. Consider the musical setting, "Renewal of Baptismal Promises" found in *Who Calls You by Name*, volume I, by David Haas.
204. See OBC, 148 and 149.

godmother (or by the godfather). If the Baptism is by immersion, the child is lifted from the sacred font by the same people.[205]

While the Baptisms take place, the community is invited to sing an acclamation or a hymn, to read from Scripture, or to observe silence. Preparation teams will want to discern how the community can best participate in the rite.

Since an ordained minister is not presiding, the anointing after Baptism is omitted. In its place is a prayer "on behalf of the newly baptized."[206] If there is more than one child baptized at a single liturgy, the prayer is said only once, and the assembly replies with "Amen." This prayer makes explicit that the newly baptized have been freed from sin and share in the priestly, prophetic, and kingly ministry of Christ, the Anointed One.

The child is then clothed with the white garment and the parents and godparents receive the lighted candle just as in the other froms of the rite. Once each family has received the baptismal candle, the catechist invites the community, especially the parents and godparents, to process to the altar.

Conclusion of the Rite

Once everyone has gathered in front of the altar, the catechist stands in front of the altar and addresses the parents and the godparents about what the child will one day receive in the Sacraments of Confirmation and the Eucharist. If appropriate, the catechist can adapt the text that is found in the rite to emphasize this connection more strongly and attempt to clarify for the assembly their baptismal responsibility to mission. The community's position in the sanctuary and placement around the altar is significant. The baptized who approach the altar week after week and who have been called to accompany the newly baptized on the journey of faith, bring the child(ren) to the altar, the place where initiation is renewed and professed each time one receives the Eucharist. The altar, a symbol of Christ, is where heaven meets earth, where our weekly gathering renews us in faith and forms us for mission. Many people do not often have an opportunity to enter the sanctuary or even stand this close to the altar. This can be a profound time for brief catechesis, but ultimately, what is said should ultimately lead the assembly into the recitation of the Lord's Prayer.

---

205. OBC, 148.
206. OBC, 151.

After the Lord's Prayer, the catechist leads the final blessing upon the assembly and then all are dismissed. Although it is not articulated in the *Order of Baptism of Children,* the rites found in *Sunday Celebrations in the Absence of a Priest* provide good guidance for how a lay minister is to preside over the Concluding Rites. While saying the customary formula "Go in peace," there is no ritual gesture.[207] The liturgy may conclude with a song that expresses "paschal joy and thanksgiving" or it may be a "Canticle of the Blessed Virgin Mary, the *Magnificat.*"[208] This song, if used, is a great way to reinforce all that has been celebrated and also affirm the call of the baptized to be missionary disciples.

Order of Baptism of Children in Danger of Death, or at the Point of Death, to Be Used in the Absence of a Priest or Deacon

The rite found in chapter V of the *Order of Baptism of Children* is to be used for baptizing children in danger of death when a deacon or priest is not available. Any suitable member of the Church or any person who has the right intention can baptize a child; for example, a trained catechist or another layperson familiar with the rite.[209] Since they are often on the front lines, parishes might consider training nurses, physicians, police officers, and other healthcare workers who live within the parish territory to administer Baptism in emergencies. These persons can be a tremendous asset to the parish community, especially if they know how to administer the sacrament properly at these difficult times. Parents or other family members may also baptize. It may be surprising to some, but even members of other Christian denominations as well as non-Christians can baptize in emergencies if they have the "right intention,"[210] especially when they are honoring the wishes of the family. Right intention means that the person who baptizes intends to do what the Church does when she baptizes (using proper matter and form). In these circumstances, "it is desirable that the minister, if possible, has one or even a second witness present."[211]

---

207. See, for example, SCAP, 149 and 214.
208. OBC, 156.
209. See OBC, 157; CI, 16.
210. CCL, 861 §2.
211. OBC, 164.

Parish preparation teams should discuss the appropriate times or circumstances in which this form of the rite is used (that is, who is most likely to be in a position to need to administer emergency Baptism, possible circumstances when they would need to do so, and how to provide those people with necessary training and catechesis about the rite). They should also discuss training all of the faithful in the proper administration of the sacrament in case they are ever confronted with this situation. When the phrase "danger of death" is used, many people presume it refers to any newborn or recently born child whose health is unstable and there is uncertainty that the child will survive. These children are often in the intensive care unit or have experienced trauma during delivery. This is certainly a common scenario; however, pastoral ministers must consider the nature of our changing world—those who live in or come from war-torn areas, those in abusive homes in which a child is put in danger, those in the midst of religious persecution, and older children who may develop an immediate life-threatening illness or may be involved in some type of accident and were not baptized as an infant.

When a child is in danger of death, he or she "is to be baptized without delay."[212] The *Code of Canon Law* states: "an infant of Catholic parents or even of non-Catholic parents is baptized licitly in danger of death even against the will of the parents."[213] While it may be permitted, pastoral ministers must carefully discern and use discretion in this circumstance in order to "[avoid] scandal and hatred of the faith."[214] In emergency situations, it may be that a minister only has time to pour water upon the child's head "with the appropriate words"[215] or "if it is prudently judged that there is sufficient time"[216] to use a fuller ritual, the rite found in chapter V of the *Order of Baptism of Children* is used.[217]

---

212. OBC, 8.1; See also CCL, 867 §2.
213. CCL, 868 §2.
214. Huels, p. 630
215. OBC, 163; see also, OBC, 164 and OBC, 21 §1.
216. OBC, 21 §2.
217. See also page 106 concerning emergencies presided over by a priest or deacon. "At the point of death or, when death is imminent and time is pressing, the minister, omitting everything else, pours water (not necessarily blessed, but natural water) over the head of the child, reciting the customary formula" (see OBC, 21).

Outline of the Rite
- Water is prepared
- Prayer of the Faithful
- Concluding prayer
- Profession of Faith
- Baptism
- [Clothing with a white garment]
- Lord's Prayer

Outline of the Rite in Extreme Emergencies (Short Form)[218]
- Water is prepared
- Baptism

The rite found in the *Order of Baptism of Children* begins with the instruction to prepare water for the rite and to gather people. If possible, the minister may want to gather a small group of people (family, friends, and hospital staff) for the short liturgy. Ensuring the presence of a small assembly highlights that it is Christ through the presence of his Church who baptizes and accompanies children on their journey and, in this case, supports the parents and family. Minimally, the minister who presides over an emergency Baptism only needs to have water, even if it is not blessed. The water can be from a sink in the room or restroom; it can even come from a bottle of water. The rite does not provide words of welcome or a greeting. However, if it seems appropriate (and if there is time), especially if the minister does not know the family, it is wise to give a brief introduction and invite those present to be mindful they are in the presence of God. Once the group has assembled, the prayer leader begins the intercessions provided in the rite. It should be noted that the usual prompt or cue ("we pray to the Lord") alerting the gathered faithful to respond, "Lord, hear our prayer," is not found in the ritual text. If the group is unchurched, the minister may be the one who leads that response. The minister could also ask the assembly to join in the response as they feel comfortable. Because there will be a lot of emotion during this liturgy, it may be difficult for those gathered to respond fully and participate verbally. Their presence and silent participation in the prayer is the greater witness. Certainly, those who are able and willing should be encouraged to participate fully.

---

218. This is not found in the OBC; instead see *Pastoral Care of the Sick*.

A lengthy but beautiful prayer concludes the intercessions. Although this prayer does not bless the water, it emphasizes the loving nature of God as the Father who gives strength and comfort to the anxious parents during this time of deep turmoil. The prayer points to the waters of Baptism as the source of eternal life by which their child will one day "obtain the inheritance"[219] of eternal life granted by his own son.

Following the prayer, the minister invites those who have assembled to profess their faith in either question or answer form or by reciting the Apostles' Creed. In this form of the rite, there is no Renunciation of Sin. If those who have gathered are unchurched and are unable to profess their faith, the lay minister may recite the Apostles' Creed on their behalf. After the Profession of Faith, the lay minister baptizes the child. Use as much water as you can provided that it is both safe for the child and permitted by those in charge of his or her medical and familial care. Let the symbol of the water bath speak—even in emergencies! The rite specifically says to pour water on the child. Pastoral ministers should not dab or trace the cross on the child's forehead with the water.

After the child is baptized, he or she may be clothed in a white garment. The garment can be a family heirloom, a newly purchased garment, or one provided by the parish or hospital. The godparents, family, and even the hospital staff can be very helpful in securing the garment as well as helping clothe the child if that is allowed. Since the white garment is a symbol of the child's Baptism—the garment of salvation—this garment could be the same in which the child is clothed in at burial. Be intentional as the words are prayed and the child is dressed. This is an opportunity for healing and consolation for the family. The other ceremonies that usually take place at this time (the Explanatory Rites: postbaptismal anointing, lighting of the baptismal candle, and *ephphatha* prayer) are omitted. The rite concludes with the Lord's Prayer. There is no final blessing or dismissal. It may seem appropriate to allow the family to remain in silent prayer or to leave in silence.

In some situations, there may not be a person who is familiar with this rite and capable of leading it. In such cases, the rite prescribes that after reciting the Apostles' Creed (which may be omitted if necessary) the water is poured over the child's head "with the appropriate words."[220] The child may

---

219. OBC, 158.
220. OBC, 163.

also be baptized "at the moment of death"[221] with simply the pouring of water "while saying the appropriate words."[222]

Emergency Baptism When a Priest or Deacon Is Available

It is interesting to note that the *Order of Baptism of Children* does not include an emergency rite for use by priests or deacons. Of course, the rituals for administering the sacraments of initiation for the dying are found in *Pastoral Care of the Sick: Rites of Anointing and Viaticum* and the newly revised *Order of Confirmation*. *Pastoral Care of the Sick* includes the Rites for Baptism, Confirmation, and the giving of Viaticum. The *Order of Confirmation* includes the updated texts for Confirmation to Be Administered to a Sick Person in Danger of Death. *Pastoral Care of the Sick* notes:

> As far as possible, the [*Order of Baptism of Children*] and the [*Order of Confirmation*] are celebrated in the usual way. The eucharist completes the sacraments of initiation. A dying child with the use of reason shares the common responsibility of receiving viaticum. It is also desirable that an even younger child complete his or her initiation by reception of the eucharist, in accord with the practice of the Church.[223]

Likewise, the *Order of Confirmation* specifies that "in the case of a child who has not reached the age of reason, Confirmation is conferred in accord with the same principles and norms laid down for the conferral of Baptism."[224] An infant does not receive Viaticum, but he or she may receive the Sacrament of Confirmation. If a deacon presides because a priest is not available, he may only administer Baptism and Viaticum (if the child is old enough to receive the Eucharist).

Although the rite found in chapter V of the *Order of Baptism of Childrenn* is typically used when a priest or deacon is not available, this does not exclude priests or deacons from using this rite. The rite notes:

> A Priest or Deacon may also use the shorter Order, if necessary, in imminent danger of death. Moreover, the pastor of the parish or other Priest possessing the same faculty, if he has the sacred Chrism at hand

---

221. OBC, 164.
222. OBC, 164.
223. PCS, 280.
224. OC, 52.

and time permits, should not fail to administer Confirmation after the Baptism. In this case the post-baptismal anointing with Chrism is omitted.[225]

Ministerial Opportunities

When an infant or child is near death, a minister meets a family in terrible trauma. Families request Baptism because they know that the child's earthly life will likely end prematurely, and they desire for their child to be baptized into the faith before approaching death. In particular, the death of the very young are the most difficult for those present, including the medical staff and ministers. Be aware of emotions and sensitivities that run quite high in such situations. A minister should also be aware of how his or her own emotions may impact their ministry.

Have awareness of the situation at hand. Learn the child's name, and whether he or she is conscious. Inquire about the family, and learn if they are able to be with their sick child. In the case of a neonate (newborn under four weeks), ask about the mother's condition. In some cases, a mother's life may still be in grave danger and may need to be anointed by a priest. Other mothers may be recovering from caesarean births, which, although common in the United States, are major abdominal surgeries that bring mothers unanticipated pain and dependence on others. To assure a recovering mother's presence at the rite, coordination with medical staff may be necessary. Additionally, it is helpful to know whether the child's illness is long-term or a new development; indeed, in non-sacramental ministry, the telling of this story may be important to the child and his or her family members. Expect the family members to have signs of shock and grief, and meet them in that sorrowful place.

When first meeting a child and his or her family, greet people by name when possible. Refer to the child by his or her name instead of using general terms like "the girl," or "the baby." Be sure to recognize the relationship the child has to others present—recognize that he or she is a son or daughter, a niece or nephew, or a grandchild. Reference his or her life, and in the case of a newborn baby, reference the child's life in the womb, the anticipation for his or her arrival, and the joy the parents knew in their child's existence. These parents have had precious little time to come to know their child, and may not have even held their sick babies. Much of their time may have been consumed with tests and worsening outcomes.

---

225. OBC, 22.

When parents inquire about Baptism, assure them that the sacrament can be provided for their child. Some families may not understand that a lay minister (or even a non-Catholic or non-Christian) can baptize their child. Catechesis may be necessary, and it can be given in a kind manner, respecting the experience of the child's family. Tell them about the rite to be celebrated, letting them know what to expect, and affirming their assent to the rite. If the child is older and still conscious, engage him or her in the conversation. Even if the child is not conscious, address him or her directly, and tell the child what his or her parents have chosen on his or her behalf. Before, during, and after the rite, as allowed by the time and situation, be present with the family, recognizing the unique reality of death's terrible suffering and pain, and Baptism's joy and promise.

It can be challenging to create a prayerful environment in a hospital. If possible, dim the flourescent lights or light a desk lamp with a warmer bulb. Place a cross or crucifix in the room. Lit candles are prohibited almost everywhere in a hospital because of the oxygen supply in the walls. If a candle is lit near a person on oxygen, the lungs could burn from the oxygen being near the flame; there is also potential for explosions and fire. Hospitals are equipped with a chapel, and depending upon the immediate need for Baptism, it might be possible for the rite to take place there, and some parents might request this. In most cases, Baptism taking place in a chapel is the exception and is most likely used in cases in which the child is born into hospice care and a fatal diagnosis is known prenatally. Often the issue is making sure the mother is able to attend the Baptism. Because of health reasons of her own related to a difficult birth, she may not be able to make the trip to the chapel and would prefer for the Baptism to take place in the NICU (neonatal intensive care unit).

If the baby is in an Isolette, ministers might ask hospital staff whether the child can be placed on an open air bed so that the baby can be baptized with ease and the parents can participate in the Baptism as much as possible. A nurse should always assist when holding a baby on a ventilator or oscillator. Ministers should never remove any medical equipment.

Because the Baptism will involve touching an ill child, ministers should follow the sanitary protocol recommended for any other healthcare worker, and if in doubt, speak to a registered nurse on the unit (not a CNA [certified nursing assistant] or simply any other person in scrubs). Ministers should always, of course, consult with hospital staff about other rules and regulations that must be followed.

Order of Bringing a Baptized Child to the Church

The Order of Bringing a Baptized Child to the Church was "drawn up for the sole case of a child baptized in danger of death";[226] in other words, it is for when a child was baptized outside of the church in an emergency situation, but has survived and is being brought to the church. In addition, the rite "may be adapted to other needs, e.g., if children have been baptized in time of religious persecution or temporary disagreement between the parents."[227] This injunction is later repeated at the end of the rite itself, and the rite should be adapted to the particular circumstances of the child, no matter what the "other difficulties"[228] prevented the celebration of Baptism in the church.

Regardless of the circumstances, it is truly a happy, blessed moment: a baptized child who was thought not to have long to live or was born into difficult circumstances has not only survived, but is now able to be welcomed by the Church. Even though the rite is rarely used, it is powerful and joyful. It should be celebrated fully whenever it occurs—with all the care that any of the baptismal rites should receive.

Like the other rites included in the *Order of Baptism of Children*, the presumption is that it will be led by a priest or deacon and take place without Mass. It also presumes that there will just be one child present, although it is possible to have more than one child in the event of the birth of multiple children or after a time of religious persecution. However, the number of children should in no way affect the joy and care with which the rite is celebrated. When celebrated without Mass, hospitality ministers should be present to welcome and provide assistance; musicians, readers, servers, and sacristans should also be there to carry out their ministries. Parishioners should also be invited to attend—during announcements at Mass, in the bulletin, social media, and through whatever forms of communication a parish uses. A brief explanation of the purpose of the rite should be included so that parishioners can understand why it is being celebrated.

The rite includes neither a provision for nor a prohibition against celebrating it during Mass. If the rite is celebrated during Mass—which could

---

226. OBC, 31 §3.
227. OBC, 31 §3.
228. OBC, 185.

easily be done—it makes sense to follow the prescribed guidelines for celebrating Baptism during Mass regarding the readings and the incorporation of the various ritual elements. Celebrating the rite during Mass not only allows the community to share in the joy of welcoming a new member, but it also serves as a catechetical moment for celebrating a rite that many Catholics do not know even exists.

The rite does not mention the font or use of water. The omission likely reflects the desire to leave no doubt that this is *not* a celebration of Baptism. While some may be tempted to sprinkle all who have gathered with holy water or to celebrate the rite around the font, it is best to avoid these practices. The child has already been baptized, and even the slightest appearance of "rebaptism" should be avoided.

The Rite of Bringing a Baptized Child to the Church includes the majority of elements that would have been omitted when the Rite of Baptism for Children in Danger of Death was celebrated.

Outline of the Rite
- Reception of the Child
    - [Song]
    - Gathering at doors of the church [or other place in church]
    - Informal greeting and welcome
    - Questioning of the parents and godparents
    - Signing of the children's forehead with the cross
    - Entrance procession/song
- Sacred Celebration of the Word of God
    - Readings [one or more[229]]
    - Homily
    - Universal Prayer / Litany of Saints
- Explanatory Rites
    - Anointing after Baptism
    - [Clothing with white garment]
    - Lighted candle
    - [Baptismal song]

---

229. If there is more than one reading add the singing of a Responsorial Psalm. If a Gospel is proclaimed include a sung Gospel acclamation.

- Conclusion of the Rite
    - Lord's Prayer
    - Blessing and Dismissal
    - [Closing song]
    - [Dedication of the child to the Blessed Virgin]

Reception of the Child

The rite begins with the reception of the child. The initial rubrics indicate that this celebration is one of joy. A psalm or song may be sung. The priest or deacon wears an "alb or surplice and stole, and even a cope, in a festive color," and he goes with the other ministers, be they servers or readers.[230] The rite begins at the entrance of the church, where "the parents and godparents are gathered with the child."[231] Even if the people have gathered in the pews or near the font, it is well worth explaining that the rite begins at the doors of the church—outside, weather permitting—and invite everyone to move to that location. The symbolic value of meeting outside the doors of the church and entering into the church is a very powerful experience and sign of the Christian journey.

After meeting the parents and godparents, the celebrant greets all who have gathered. The celebrant "praises them for having had the child baptized without delay, and gives thanks to God and congratulates the parents on the child's return to health."[232] These words could certainly be adapted for whatever the particular circumstances are, but the general message is one of joy—the child was baptized in a moment of great difficulty and trial, and now, the Church rejoices in being able to celebrate that Baptism.

The celebrant then asks the parents (or, if culturally appropriate, the godparents) what name they have given the child. He continues by asking, "Since he (she) has already been baptized, what do you now as of God's Church for **N.**?" In the text, the suggested responses are "That in the presence of the community it may be known that he (she) has been received into the Church" or "that he (she) is a Christian" or "that he (she) has been baptized."[233] The parents should be prepared for this question. Allowing the parents to answer

---

230. See OBC, 165.
231. OBC, 165.
232. OBC, 166.
233. OBC, 167.

for themselves is powerful, as it invites them to declare why they have brought their child to participate in this rite.

The reception of the child concludes with the usual questioning of the parents and godparents and with the tracing of the Sign of the Cross on the child's forehead by the celebrant, parents, and "if it seems appropriate," the godparents. The celebrant then invites all who are present to participate in the Liturgy of the Word. There may be a procession to the place where the Liturgy of the Word will occur, and if so, Psalm 84 (85) or another psalm or song may be sung. This is the only procession included in this particular rite; there is no need to process to the baptistry because no Baptism will occur.

Sacred Celebration of the Word of God

There are several options for where the celebration of the Word could take place: in a narthex or gathering space, in the pews, in the main body of the church, and even at the entrance of the church where the reception of the child occurred. The rite says that "all are seated."[234]

The rite offers a sparse, highly flexible outline for the celebration of the Word. The first part consists of the readings and the homily. Four Gospel readings are provided (John 3:1–6; Matthew 28:18–20; Mark 1:9–11; and Mark 10:13–16). One, or even two, of these Gospel readings may be proclaimed. The rite also provides options from the Old Testament (both 1 and 2 Kings) and any of the readings found in chapter VII of the rite may be used. Passages such as 1 Kings 17:17–24 (Elijah prays to God, who restores life to a child who had stopped breathing) or 2 Kings 4:8–37 (Elisha prays to God, who restores life to a child who had stopped breathing) may also be chosen if they meet the "needs of the parents."[235] Responsorial Psalms may be chosen to come between the readings.

The personalization of this liturgy continues in the "brief homily," when the celebrant can reflect on the readings and offer insight into Baptism and the responsibilities that the parents and godparents are assuming.

The goal of this remarkable ritual flexibility is to enable the Church to celebrate as intimately as possible with the family. Knowing the family and their particular circumstances, the celebrant should be able to guide the selection of readings that speak to the personal situation of the child who is being welcomed. For families, hearing a specific Scripture reading that speaks

---

234. OBC, 172.
235. OBC, 172.

directly to their experience and situation is especially powerful. It helps to connect their lived experience of God and their child's seemingly miraculous recovery with that of their forebears in faith.

After the homily, the celebrant may lead all in a period of silent prayer, or a hymn may be sung. The Universal Prayer and the Litany of the Saints follows. The intercessions given in the rite are very basic; they ask for the child to be "mindful of his (her) Baptism and restoration to health" to "come with joy to the table of [Christ's] sacrifice," to "grow in holiness and wisdom," and so forth.[236] These petitions can and should be adapted to the particular situation by using the other forms of the intercessions provided in the rite as a model. At the very least, it is advisable to add "we pray to the Lord" or a similar invitation at the end of each petition so that the assembly may easily respond. The response may be chanted if appropriate, and the celebrant should inform the people of the response prior to the first petition (or it may be printed in the worship aid to avoid annoucements during the liturgy).

After the petitions, the celebrant invites the assembly to join in the praying of the Litany of the Saints. No words are given for the invitation, so a brief introduction inviting the assembly to respond with "pray for us" is appropriate. Only a few saints are listed in the ritual text; other saints may be added. The rite suggests adding the patrons of the child, the parish, or local diocese. Other family members' patrons, the saint of the day, or other significant saints may also be included. The litany ends with "All holy men and women, Saints of God, pray for us."[237] After the litany the celebrant prays a closing prayer which can be adapted; although the prayer provided in the ritual text is approriate for many situations.

Explanatory Rites

In the other forms of the baptismal rites, the Profession of Faith and the Baptism would take place at this point in the ritual. Because the child has already been baptized, these parts are omitted. Instead, the rite continues with the Explanatory Rites that were omitted when the child was baptized: the anointing after Baptism, the clothing with the white garment, and the presentation of the lighted candle. These elements take place as they would during the baptismal rite. One of the acclamations found in chapter VII may be sung during the handing on of the candle. In the other rites, this

---

236. OBC, 175.
237. OBC, 176.

acclamation immediately follows the Baptism. Its placement here is a fitting, joyful conclusion to the Explanatory Rites.

Conclusion of the Rite

The rite concludes with the Lord's Prayer, final blessing, and the dismissal. This portion of the rite proceeds exactly as it does in the other rites of Baptism that are celebrated by a priest or a deacon, including the closing song, and the optional devotional practice of presenting the newly "baptized infant to the altar of the Blessed Virgin Mary."[238]

Other Important Pastoral Considerations

Liturgical Music

In their 2007 document, *Sing to the Lord: Music in Divine Worship*, the United States bishops affirmed the importance of music in all liturgical celebrations. Music helps us experience God's presence in a deeper way both individually and communally.[239] "Singing together in church expresses so well the sacramental presence of God to his people."[240] Music "strengthens our faith when it grows weak and draws us into the divinely inspired voice of the Church at prayer."[241]

> Music is a way for God to lead us to the realm of higher things.
> —*Sing to the Lord: Music in Divine Worship*, 2

The musical voice of "the Church at prayer" is most powerfully manifest during Mass—especially on Sundays. In a 1998 pastoral letter, St. John Paul II noted that "the *dies Domini* is also the *dies Ecclesiae*": the day of the Lord is the day of the Church.[242] When Sunday Mass is celebrated with joy and solemnity, with the whole community gathered on the day of the Lord's Resurrection, "it becomes the paradigm for other Eucharistic celebrations."[243] He goes on to say that music, particularly singing, is essential for Sunday Mass because it is "a particularly apt way to express a joyful heart, accentuating the solemnity of the celebration and fostering the sense of a common faith

---

238. OBC, 184.
239. See STL, 2.
240. STL, 2.
241. STL, 5.
242. DD, 35.
243. DD, 34.

and a shared love."²⁴⁴ For all of these reasons, music is an indispensable element of Sunday Mass—and the time and dedication that many parishes put into preparing music reflects its importance.

Sunday Mass is the paradigm not only for all Eucharistic celebrations, but for all of the times the Church gathers to pray. The Mass is not the only way that the Church prays, and the same care that goes into preparing music for Mass should guide the decision-making process for the other rites and devotions of the Church, including the Sacrament of Baptism. Singing is essential whenever the Church, both within and outside Mass, celebrates the sacraments. The sacramental rites themselves prescribe and presume that there will be singing. *Sing to the Lord* emphasizes the need for parishes to recall "the importance of singing envisioned by these rites,"²⁴⁵ and the document provides guidance for incorporating music into the Christian initiation of adults, Confirmation, Ordination, Marriage, Anointing of the Sick, Penance, and Baptism for children.²⁴⁶ The music that is selected for these sacramental rites, including Baptisms for children, should "foster and nourish faith."²⁴⁷

Musical Roles

Most importantly, everybody who is present for Baptism has a musical role to play. The priest "sings the presidential prayers and dialogues . . . according to his capabilities,"²⁴⁸ and the deacon sings the dialogues, invitations, and any other "parts of the Liturgy that belong" to him.²⁴⁹ The assembly (including the priest and the deacon) sings "acclamations, responses, psalms, antiphons [and] hymns."²⁵⁰ Most likely, other music ministers (choir, cantor, psalmist, organist, instrumentalists, and music director) will be present for Baptisms during Mass. For Baptisms without Mass, the number and type of music ministers should reflect the best that a given parish can provide—certainly at least one with "the skill of leading unaccompanied singing,"²⁵¹ but also more when at all possible. The leadership of a singing celebrant and the presence of music

---

244. DD, 50.
245. STL, 207.
246. See STL, 200–229.
247. STL, 5.
248. STL, 19. The documents of the postconciliar liturgical renewal repeatedly commend the ideal of a sung Liturgy with sung dialogues between priest and people, such as *The Lord be with you*, the acclamation at the end of the Gospel, and the introductory dialogue to the Eucharistic Prayer. See *Musicam sacram*, 29–31; *Lectionary for Mass (Second Typical Edition): Introduction* (LFM), 17; GIRM, 40.
249. STL, 23.
250. STL, 26; quoting CSL, 30.
251. STL, 207.

ministers both inspire the assembly to sing and contribute to the festivity of the celebration.

Musical Elements of the Rite

Sing to the Lord identifies four different categories that appear both in Sunday Mass and in the *Order of Baptism of Children*:

1. *Dialogues and Acclamations*: These elements are "fundamental" to the liturgy and are "short and uncomplicated and easily invite active participation by the entire assembly."[252] This includes the greetings ("The Lord be with you / And with your spirit"); prayer formulas ("Through Christ our Lord / Amen"); an Alleluia or other acclamation that may be sung prior to the Gospel; an acclamation that may be sung after the Profession of Faith; and an acclamation (an Alleluia or another appropriate response) that can be sung immediately after each child is baptized. Ideally, musical settings of the dialogues and acclamations should be so familiar because of usage at Sunday Mass that they can be easily sung at all Baptisms, whether accompanied or a cappella.

2. *Antiphons and Psalms*: The psalms have long been "the basic songbook of the Liturgy."[253] In the *Order of Baptism of Children*, psalms may be sung as a responsorial psalm after a reading and during the various processions (at the beginning of the rite, before the Liturgy of the Word, after the Liturgy of the Word, and before the Lord's Prayer at the conclusion of the rite). There are also a number of Scripture-based antiphons that may be used.

3. *Refrains and Repeated Responses*: These include "texts of a litanic character"[254] that have a short, repeated response. During the baptismal rites, these texts include the responses to the Universal Prayer ("Let us pray to the Lord / Lord, hear our prayer"), the Litany of the Saints ("St. N. /Pray for us"), and optional responsory forms of the blessing and invocation of God over baptismal water (the congregation responds with "Blessed be God" or a similar response after each statement made by the celebrant).

4. *Hymns*: The *Order of Baptism of Children* indicates that hymns may be sung when the people gather at the beginning of the rite, during

the procession after the reception of the children, after the homily, and at the conclusion of the rite. If a large number of children are being baptized, hymns may also be sung during the Baptisms themselves.[255] Scripture-based hymn texts and other texts are provided in chapter VII of the rite, but other appropriate hymns may also be chosen. When Baptism is celebrated during Mass, hymns or other songs may also be sung during the Preparation of the Gifts and the reception of Communion.

In addition to these parts of the liturgy, the Lord's Prayer may also be sung. The priest celebrant may choose to chant the other parts of the Mass, that is the Collect, Eucharistic Prayer, Prayer over the Offerings, and the Prayer after Communion.

Citing the *General Instruction of the Roman Missal*, *Sing to the Lord* urges that when choosing what to sing from among the various options, "preference should be given to those [parts] that are of greater importance."[256] Ideally, the dialogues should be sung at all Baptisms. As for the other elements, the specific antiphons, psalms, refrains, and hymns that are chosen will depend upon the specific pastoral setting. Just as when choosing music for Sunday Mass, parish preparation teams should ask these questions based upon the three main judgments identified by *Sing to the Lord*:

- Is it appropriate for the liturgical action? (the liturgical)
- Is it appropriate and capable for this particular assembly? (the pastoral)
- Is it aesthetically worthy? (the musical)[257]

Finally, *Sing to the Lord* identifies several logistical concerns that should be considered in order to facilitate musical participation. Music ministers should be located "so as to enable proper interaction with the liturgical action, with the rest of the assembly, and among the various musicians."[258] Architectural and acoustical properties that encourage or inhibit singing should be considered,[259] especially given that the *Order of Baptism of Children* incorporates processions and takes place in different acoustical zones of the church (the font, baptistry, church entrance, and sanctuary). In addition to being a catechetical tool, the use of hymnals or well-designed worship aids can

---

255. See OBC, 150.
256. STL, 115; quoting GIRM, 40.
257. See STL, 126–136.
258. STL, 95.
259. See STL, 101–104.

facilitate the assembly's sung and spoken participation.[260] When parishes create their own worship aids, they should follow their "legal and moral obligation to seek proper permissions"[261] before reprinting text and music. All of these are topics that can be addressed by baptismal preparation teams well in advance of the celebration of the sacrament.

One final note: because liturgical music is the joyful, authentic, sung prayer of the gathered people, the use of recorded music should be avoided.[262]

Liturgical Environment

The most important visual symbols in a church should be the focal points of a liturgical celebration. These "primary liturgical points of focus" should always be central, and any additional decorations should "draw people to the true nature of the mystery being celebrated rather than being ends in themselves."[263] During Sunday Mass, for example, the ambo and altar are the primary points of focus for the Liturgy of the Word and the Liturgy of the Eucharist. When additional decorations or adornments are used, they should draw attention to those points of focus—not obscure or distract from them.

Similarly, the liturgical environment for Baptism should emphasize the "primary liturgical points of focus"[264] for the celebration of the sacrament. Any additional decorations and adornments beyond what is already in place for Mass should draw attention to these primary baptismal symbols: the font and its water, the Paschal candle, and the oils/ambry.

The Baptismal Font

Without question, the central element of the liturgical environment for Baptism is the font. It is the one liturgical object explicitly mentioned in both of the praenotanda. The *Order of Baptism of Children* states:

> In order that Baptism may be seen more clearly as the Sacrament of the Church's faith and of incorporation into the People of God, it should normally be celebrated in the parish church, which ought to have a baptismal font.[265]

---

260. See also pages 41, 50, 56, 79, 114, 124, and 145.
261. STl, 105.
262. See STL, 93.
263. BLS, 124.
264. BLS, 124.
265. OBC, 10.

Christian Initiation, General Introduction, urges that the font should be clean and beautiful.

Built of Living Stones, the 2000 document of the United States Conference of Catholic Bishops, provides guidance for the construction and renovation of churches. In regards to the baptismal font, the document emphasizes that because Baptism and Eucharist are both sacraments of initiation the font and its location should "reflect the Christian's journey *through* the waters of baptism *to* the altar."[266] In order to convey this connection, the document recommends placing the altar and the font on the same axis and use similar lighting, floor patterns, materials, and other design elements. The document also notes that whether the font is in the main body of the church or in a separate baptistry, it "should be visible and accessible to all who enter the church building."[267] The document also stresses that the font is "a symbol of both tomb and womb, its power is the power of the triumphant cross; and baptism sets the Christian on the path to life that will never end, the 'eighth day' of eternity where Christ's reign of peace and justice is celebrated"[268] and use of traditional symbolism will emphasize these theological points (for example, steps to symbolize descent into a tomb, crosses adorning the baptistery, or an eight-sided font or baptistery area to symbolize the eighth day).

Built of Living Stones encourages that fonts be constructed so that they accommodate the Baptism of both adults and infants, with ample water for both immersion and pouring. By its location and surroundings, the font should facilitate congregational participation in the Order of Baptism. If near the entrance to the church, the font should invite reflection on the relationship between Baptism and the other sacraments and milestones of the Christian life. Lastly, there should

> The rites of baptism, the first of the sacraments of initiation, require a prominent place for celebration. Initiation into the Church is entrance into a eucharistic community united in Jesus Christ. Because the rites of initiation of the Church begin with baptism and are completed by the reception of the Eucharist, the baptismal font and its location reflect the Christian's journey *through* the waters of baptism *to* the altar.
>
> —*Built of Living Stones,* 66; referencing the *Rite of Christian Initiation of Adults,* 25

---

266. BLS, 66.
267. BLS, 67.
268. BLS, 68.

be private locations nearby for the newly baptized adults (not children) to be clothed in white garments.[269]

Accesibility of the Font

The font's centrality during Baptism speaks most powerfully if it is a central symbol of the liturgical environment throughout the year. Although the placement, size, and style of fonts vary widely from place to place, several general principles apply. If the font is in the gathering space, narthex, or entrance of the church make sure that it is visible to the assembly keeping a visual axis to the altar and that people can gather around it freely for the celebration of Baptism. Be careful not to block the font with flowers (such as poinsettias and lilies) during Christmas and Easter Time; the font should always be accessible.

Above all, if the font is in an accessible location near the main entrance of the church, keep it open throughout the year. Let the font be the central gathering point as people enter the church to allow them to bless themselves with holy water. If the font is accessible from all entrances, it makes neither symbolic nor ritual sense to cover the primary font and use smaller holy water fonts instead. When multiple entrances to the church do necessitate smaller fonts near the doors, they should be clearly visible and (if possible) linked to the primary font by design or materials.

In places where keeping the font covered when a Baptism is not taking place is usually a nonnegotiable practice, consider whether it is possible to open the main font on the weekends for Sunday Masses so that the assembly can sign themselves from the waters of the font when they enter the church for Mass—especially if a Baptism will take place within or outside Mases that weekend. In addition to intercessions and bulletin announcements, the liturgical environment therefore speaks for itself: "A Baptism is happening soon (or has just happened). Alleluia!"

Keep water in the font throughout the year including during Lent. The only time the font should be emptied is during the Sacred Paschal Triduum. Fonts are emptied following the evening Mass of the Lord's Supper on Holy Thursday and they are refilled for the baptismal liturgy that will take place during the Easter Vigil. If possible, sprinkle holy water directly from the font onto the casket or coffin during the funeral rites. The same water that

---

269. See BLS, 69.

symbolizes death and rebirth in Baptism also marks the transition from earthly death to eternal life.

Running Water

Many newer fonts, particularly those that allow for immersion of adults and children, have the option for a continuously flowing water supply. If this is an option in your parish, keep the water running as much as possible. Theologically, bubbling water echoes the many Scripture texts that emphasize the movement of water. There is also a practical benefit to moving water: even though the font will still need to be cleaned periodically, the water circulation helps to inhibit the growth of mold and algae.[270]

> I saw water flowing from the Temple, from its right-hand side, alleluia: and all to whom this water came were saved and shall say: Alleluia, alleluia.
>
> —*Vidi aquam*, The Roman Missal, Easter Vigil

Bowls

Since the Second Vatican Council, a renewed theological emphasis on the Baptism of adults and children (who have reached the age of reason) has led to an increase in the number of large, immersion-ready fonts. However, many parishes still maintain the use of bowl or bowl-on-pedestal fonts, which may date back decades and even centuries. Doing so maintains a sense of historical continuity, as babies are often baptized in the same font as their parents, grandparents, and prior generations.

If your parish's font is a bowl, make sure that both the bowl (and, if required, its stand) are as heavy, solid, and permanent as possible. It is wonderful when the design or materials match the altar. If they do not, consider making a small fabric parament from the same material as the altar cloth in order to link the font visually with the altar. As opposed to larger fonts, which generally do not need to have visual attention called to themselves, smaller fonts may need additional lighting, alternate flooring, or another means of demarcating them from their surroundings, particularly if they are in a crowded sanctuary or the corner of a busy gathering space. The overarching principle is the same: highlight the font.

While the use of a permanent font is preferable, occasionally a font bowl and stand may be moved to a temporary location in the front of the church

---

270. For example, the river flowing in Psalm 46 or the water flowing from the Temple in Ezekiel 47.

to facilitate participation of all who are gathered for the Baptism. This adaptation should only be made when "the baptistery is unable to accommodate all catechumens or all of those present."[271] When this is the case, the same principles apply: make it appear as permanent as possible (no rickety tables or shaky stands) and make sure that it is visible to all.

Other Liturgical Symbols

Regarding the other symbols of Baptism, the Paschal candle should be placed solidly in its holder and clearly lit. Outside of Easter Time (when it belongs near the ambo or in the sanctuary) and funerals (when it belongs near the coffin), the candle should reside in "a place of honor in the baptistry for use in the celebration of baptisms."[272] The flame should be visible, reachable, and easily accessible.

When Baptisms are being celebrated at a permanent font immediately following a weekend Mass, lighting the Paschal candle prior to the Mass seems to be a permissible pastoral adaptation that visually signifies that Baptisms will be occurring, thereby again linking the sacramental celebration with the gathered Church into which the child is being initiated.

As for the oils, they should generally be kept in an ambry: "a simple, dignified, and secure niche in the baptistry" free of "bright light or high temperatures"[273] that might lead to spoilage of the oils. If the ambry is nearby and the oil can be easily accessed inside the vessels, there is no need to remove the oils from the ambry prior to the Baptism. If setting up the oils in advance is necessary, they should be placed on an appropriate credence table.

Place the baptismal candles, ritual book, towels, and other items of need on the credence table, not on the font.

---

271. CI, 26.
272. BLS, 94.
273. BLS, 117.

Regardless of whether it is needed to hold the oils, a credence table is often useful for holding baptismal candles, towels, purificators, and other items. The table should be appropriately sized, suitably dignified, and sufficiently sturdy to hold everything that is necessary for the rite. If there is no server to hold the book for the priest or deacon, there may also be a stand for the book(s) so that the priest's hands are both free. If a large number of children are being baptized, several tables may be necessary, or else other provisions should be made to ensure that towels, white garments, and candles are easily accessible during the celebration of the sacrament.

Additional Decor

Just as when they are used during Sunday Mass, flowers and other plants should never hinder the celebration of the rite. However, the judicious incorporation of plants into the baptistery can add to the beauty of the liturgical environment. A few well-placed plants can help to draw attention to the font and visually link it with the other primary symbols of the church, including the altar and ambo. Traditional seasonal flowers vary from place to place (for example, lilies during the Easter Time, poinsettias during the Christmas Time, other greenery during Ordinary Time). Their use is also appropriate as long as they do not create a wall that obscures or blocks access to the font.

Multicultural Concerns

Parishes in North America should be attentive to the way Baptism is celebrated among various cultures. Parish preparation teams should make every effort to learn how those from different cultural traditions understand Baptism, the role of godparents, the rite itself, and other traditions surrounding this important event in the life of a new Christian. The primary goal for the liturgical celebration is the full, conscious, and active participation of those gathered. Considerations should be made to prepare liturgies that reflect the vision of the rite and how the rite may be legitimately adapted. Great care should also be given to the selection of music, the language of the prayers and readings,[274] the preparation of worship aids, and parish hospitality. The membership of the parish preparation team should reflect the culture of the parish. In this way, the preparation team is familiar with the different expressions of faith and diversity of the various cultures that make up the parish

---

274. In the dioceses of the United States, bilingual English and Spanish texts have been prepared and are available as a single ritual edition.

community. In order to prepare culturally appropriate music, a well-trained representative from the music ministry needs to be involved in the preparation team. The music ministry will also need to be well prepared and trained so they can effectively lead the music in different languages. All pastoral decisions should be guided by the principles that govern Sunday Mass.

Evangelization

The Baptism of children is a truly joyful sacramental rite of the Curch, and it is itself a moment for evangelization for many different groups of people.

Parents have their children baptized for many reasons. Some parents are active members of a parish who attend Mass regularly and participate in the life of the parish. Others may attend Mass sporadically, while still others have had little significant connection to a parish since their wedding, if that.

For all of these parents, Baptism is a moment for evangelization. This evangelization has a catechetical component. During the baptismal preparation process and in the rite itself, parents are invited to reflect on the meaning of Baptism: they themselves were once baptized as followers of Christ, and now they have a chance to renew their own baptismal commitments as they prepare for the Baptism of their children. For unbaptized parents, this period of catechetical preparation is particularly significant in order to help them understand what Baptism truly means. For all parents, they are invited to reflect on what it means to make their home a true domestic Church, one in which they will raise their children as faithful disciples.

Moreover, Baptism is a moment of rewelcoming. For parents who have not been as active in the parish, evangelization means talking about parish organizations, inviting them to parish events, and encouraging a deeper commitment to participation in the sacramental, service, and community life of the parish. For parents who are already active participants in parish life, Baptism is a moment of transition. Many parishes require baptismal preparation classes only for new parents or new parishioners, so evangelizing means assisting active members in moving from husband and wife to father and mother. If they have been attending young adult groups, they could be invited to young parent or young family groups. For all parents, the birth and Baptism of a child is a moment for deepening vocational understanding and strengthening the need for Christ's presence in their lives. Intentionally evangelizing and re-welcoming them is essential.

The birth of a child is an opportunity to deepen a parents' understanding of their vocation and need for Christ in their life.

This evangelization should continue after the Baptism itself. For instance, if a parish provides breakfast or coffee and doughnuts after Mass, schedule one of these events as a special day for families of all who have had children baptized in the past year. Even if they do not attend, the invitation is itself an act of evangelization. It is a reminder of their child's Baptism and of their belonging to the parish, a place where they are always welcome just as Christ welcomes each of us.

Parents can also be encouraged to celebrate the anniversary of their children's Baptism. Encourage parents to have a party, relight the baptismal candle, read a baptismal passage from Scripture, look at photos, or watch the video of the Baptism. Baptism is the beginning of new life in Christ, and celebrating every year is a powerful reminder of its importance. Parishes can provide parents with a copy of the Order of Blessing of Sons and Daughters as found in the *Book of Blessings*. Parents may preside over this ritual each year on the anniversary of their child's Baptism.[275]

---

275. The blessing is found in chapter I of the *Book of Blessings* (BB) (see BB, 174–194).

For everybody who gathers for a Baptism, participating in the rite is itself a moment of renewal and evangelization. For those who are Christian and were baptized (or had family members of their own baptized), it reminds them of their own Baptism and Baptisms in which they have participated in the past. For godparents, it is a moment in which they assume a responsibility that brings them closer to the parents of the children. For older siblings who were baptized as infants, it may be the first time that they have gotten to see and experience this event that happened to them years ago. For those who are not Catholic (or Christian), it can provide a powerful experience of how the Catholic faith is lived and embodied. For all who are visiting a parish, Baptism offers a glimpse into how this particular community lives its life as Christians.

Whether it is celebrated during or without Mass, the Order of Baptism evangelizes in many ways. Everything matters because those in attendance will notice a different symbol, word, or action and will view it through the lenses of their own experiences and personal backgrounds. This need not put undue pressure on the rite. What is most important is to convey a sense of welcome and of joy. Baptism evangelizes best when it is celebrated joyfully, with full attention, reverence, and care. Witnessing and participating in such a celebration is engaging; it draws in all who are present. When people are engaged deeply, they themselves become more open so that the Holy Spirit can move freely and transform their hearts.

Being a godparent provides a powerful experience of how the Catholic faith is lived and embodied.

The best way to convey a sense of welcome and of joy is to live it. The celebrant has a particularly important role—he welcomes all as Christ, and he represents the parish community and the universal Church. He is not alone, however. Setting up in advance conveys a sense of preparation. Being at the door to greet people and guide them conveys a sense of welcome. Being happy to be there conveys a sense that this moment is important, that there is nowhere else that a Christian would rather be. For family members, friends, and godparents—especially those who have been away from the

Church or who harbor negative feelings and attitudes—simply being in the presence of others who are moved by Christian joy is a powerfully evangelizing moment.

Many ministers have heard countless Baptism-related laments from parishioners. "Oh, Mass took forever today; there were four Baptisms." "Oh, I couldn't hear anything at Mass today because there were Baptisms after Mass and the kids kept crying." "Oh, that family whose kid was baptized today never comes to church, and they left a huge mess in the pews."

These kinds of comments reflect the need for evangelizing parishioners about Baptism. Simply put, parishioners need to understand that Baptism is important. Baptism is a sign that a parish is growing, that new life is happening. During a time when so many parishes are merging, twinning, clustering, and closing, and when so many parents choose not to have their children baptized, every Baptism needs to be celebrated and acknowledged publicly as a joy—not as a nuisance that lengthens Mass or crowds the gathering space afterwards. Whether Baptism is celebrated during or outside of Mass, it is a cause for celebration. The Church is growing! This child is initiated! Alleluia!

If a parish has a sign outside, consider using it to welcome the "newly baptized," perhaps even by first name (if space allows and with parental permission). Such a sign enables all who drive or walk by the church see that the Church is growing. That is evangelical message; it indicates that this parish is indeed fulfilling the Great Commission. Its members are making disciples of all people through baptizing, teaching, and proclaiming the Good News. The whole community sees that for this parish, its newest members are so important that they are publicly acknowledged and celebrated on the sign.

> In virtue of their baptism, all the members of the People of God have become missionary disciples (cf. Mt 28:19). All the baptized, whatever their position in the Church or their level of instruction in the faith, are agents of evangelization.
>
> —*Evangelii gaudium*, 120

The same spirit of joyful announcement applies to websites, bulletins, social media pages, and other ways the parish seeks to engage the broader community. Spread the Good News that the Good News is being spread. Inspire the making of disciples by announcing the making of disciples.

Celebrating the Baptism of children is one of the most joyful moments in the life of a parish, but it is, of course, only a beginning. In the weeks, months, and years following the celebration of Baptism, the same parish that celebrated those children's initiation assumes the responsibility of helping them to grow in faith and to live a life of discipleship. Most people who are baptized as children do not remember their own Baptism, but they do remember the Baptisms that they see and about which they hear. When they hear a priest, deacon, or catechist talk about the importance of Baptism, they will know that they too have been baptized, that they have been initiated into the Church as disciples of Jesus Christ. Over time, as they receive the other sacraments of initiation, they will come to know more deeply the call that began with their own Baptism—the call to live the Great Commission by evangelizing and making disciples, baptizing all nations in the name of the Father, the Son, and the Holy Spirit.

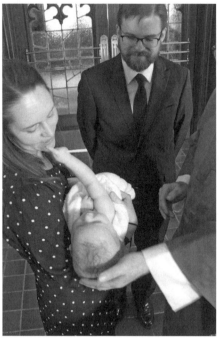

The Baptism of a child is one of the most joyous occasions in the life of a parish.

Frequently Asked Questions

1. Why is Baptism important?

Christians are baptized because Jesus himself was baptized in the Jordan River and commanded his disciples to go forth and make disciples of all nations by baptizing in the name of the Trinity.[1] Baptism is absolutely essential for anybody who wishes to be a disciple of Christ. It is, as the *Catechism of the Catholic Church* states, "the basis of the whole Christian life, the gateway to life in the Spirit . . . , and the door which gives access to the other sacraments."[2] This sacrament forgives all sins, bestows unfathomable grace, and permanently incorporates those who are baptized into the Body of Christ. Most Christian denominations consider Baptism necessary for salvation. It forever marks one for Christ as a member of his Church.

> If, then, we have died with Christ, we believe that we shall also live with him. We know that Christ, raised from the dead, dies no more; death no longer has power over him. As to his death, he died to sin once and for all; as to his life, he lives for God.
>
> —Romans 6:8–10

In Romans 6:1–11, St. Paul reminds us that Baptism has effected a very real change in baptized persons and demands they live and engage in the world differently. The one who enters the waters of Baptism intimately shares in Christ's suffering, death, and Resurrection; that is, the Paschal Mystery. The washing with water helps the community understand and witness what God's grace is doing in the new Christian. By sharing in Christ's death, the newly baptized are liberated from the darkness of sin, which had alienated them from God, and they are adopted as his sons and daughters. This same washing also symbolizes the new Christian's rebirth and inheritance of the glory of Christ's Resurrection. As the new Christian comes forth from the water, their soul—their whole being!—radiates with the newness of life and God's amazing grace. The baptized are forever changed and now share in the

---

1. See Matthew 28:19–20.
2. CCC, 1213.

priestly, prophetic, and kingly ministry of Jesus Christ.[3] Although their journey of incorporation into the Church will be completed with Confirmation and Eucharist, in Baptism they are forever united to Christ and made a member of his Body.

2. Do parents have to be registered parishioners in order to have their child baptized?

Canonically, there is no requirement that parents must be registered parishioners in order for their child to be baptized. Pastors are responsible for all Catholics (and, indeed, all people) living in the parish territory, whether they are registered members or not. That said, especially in the United States, parish registration is often seen as an expression of one's commitment to participate in the life of the parish and, for parents seeking Baptism, as evidence that their children will be raised in the faith.

Pastorally, Baptism provides an opportunity to discuss with unregistered parents why they want to have their child baptized, how they themselves are practicing their faith, how they will raise their child as a Catholic, and if they would like to become registered parishioners. However, registration should never be a litmus test preventing this evangelizing conversation from happening nor for preventing Baptism from taking place.[4]

3. Is there ever cause to deny a child Baptism?

The *Code of Canon Law* requires that two conditions be met in order for a child to be baptized: (1) at least one parent (or "person who legitimately takes their place"[5]) gives consent, and (2) there "must be a founded hope that the infant will be brought up in the Catholic religion."[6] What exactly constitutes a "founded hope" varies, but often, the parents' desire to have a child baptized and their willingness to participate in baptismal preparation serves as sufficient evidence for such hope. Very rarely is a "founded hope" completely absent, which is why there is no blanket prohibition against Baptism for specific reasons (that is, the child's familial situation or the marital status of the parents).

---

3. See *Lumen gentium*, 31.
4. See question 3 concerning the canonical requirements for infant Baptism to take place.
5. CCL, 868 §1, 1°.
6. CCL, 868 §1, 2°.

Even when "such hope is altogether lacking, the baptism is to be delayed according to the prescripts of particular law after the parents have been advised about the reason."[7] In other words, Baptism is never refused once and for all; it is delayed for reasons explained to the parents, all in the hope that those reasons can be resolved and the child can be baptized as soon as possible.

4. If a child is in danger of death, should he or she be confirmed when Baptism is celebrated?

The *Order of Baptism of Children* notes that "the pastor of the parish or other Priest possessing the same faculty, if he has the sacred Chrism at hand and time permits, should not fail to administer Confirmation after the Baptism."[8] Any priest may confirm a person (infant or adult) who is in danger of death without permission from the bishop.

If Baptism is administered by a lay person when one is in danger of death, neither the postbaptismal anointing nor Confirmation can be celebrated. After the liturgy, a lay minister may remain with the family to read Scripture, pray, or listen to the needs of the family. During this difficult time, the art of accompaniment is crucial. If Baptism is administered by a deacon when one is in danger of death, he may administer the postbaptismal anointing but he may not confirm.[9]

> The following possess the faculty of administering confirmation by the law itself:
> 1° within the boundaries of their jurisdiction, those who are equivalent in law to a diocesan bishop;
> 2° as regards the person in question, the presbyter who by virtue of office or mandate of the diocesan bishop baptizes one who is no longer an infant or admits one already baptized into the full communion of the Catholic Church; 3° as regards those who are in danger of death, the pastor or indeed any presbyter.
> —*Code of Canon Law*, 883

---

7. CCL, 868 §1, 2°.
8. OBC, 22.
9. See CCL, 883 3° and 891.

5. Can parents choose the priest or deacon who baptizes their child?

"The ordinary ministers of Baptism are Bishops, Priests, and Deacons"[10] within or without Mass. Who celebrates a particular Baptism and in what form (within Mass or without Mass) is a decision that is generally made by the pastor of the parent's parish or the pastor in consultation with the other clergy the parents would like to be involved. Requests for a specific priest or deacon (that is, a family member or a family friend either from the parish or from outside the parish) should be discussed with the pastor. If such a request is granted, documentation (that is, if the priest or deacon is a minister in good standing) and the appropriate permissions from the bishops of the local diocese and the visiting minister's diocese to celebrate the sacrament will need to be secured.

For Baptism during Masses when both a priest and deacon are present, the most common practice is that the priest performs the Baptism because he is the presider of the Mass. However, there is no explicit prohibition against a deacon performing the Baptism, and the ritual text explicitly permits deacons to baptize if there are a large number of children. Specific requests should be discussed with the pastor.

6. Is there a fee for Baptism?

As parish staffs do for Marriages and funerals, some request a fee or stipend for Baptisms. The amount may be set at the diocesan or the parish level, and it varies depending upon whether the funds are directed to the parish general fund, to the priest or deacon, to servers or musicians, or elsewhere. However, when paying a stipend is a true financial hardship for a family, Baptism should not be contingent on payment. The *Code of Canon Law* clearly states: "the minister is to seek nothing for the administration of the sacraments beyond the offerings defined by competent authority, always taking care that the needy are not deprived of the assistance of the sacraments because of poverty."[11] In places where there is no requested stipend, families may choose to make a donation to the celebrant and/or to the parish on the occasion of Baptism.

---

10. CI, 11.
11. CCL, 848.

7. Are parents required to name their children after saints?

There are many wonderful reasons for selecting a saint's or biblical name for a child, but such a name is not required for Baptism. The only canonical requirement regarding the name is that the name not be "foreign to Christian sensibility."[12] For example, names strongly associated with other, non-biblical religions—Krishna, Vishnu, or other Hindu deities, for instance—or names of demonic origin are problematic.

8. Is it necessary for the parish to provide a baptismal garment for a child?

The *Order of Baptism of Children* specifies that "it is desirable that the families themselves provide [the baptismal] garment."[13] Indeed, many children are already wearing white clothing even before the Order of Baptism begins. These clothes are usually appropriate baptismal garments; they are most often complete outfits (dresses, white pants, or shorts), suitably formal, and occasionally passed down from generation to generation. If the children are wearing such clothing, the parish does not need to provide an additional garment.

When children are not wearing white garments, a parish may provide a garment when necessary, particularly for those families who are unable to provide one on their own. Rather than a small bib-style garment, a robe or gown that completely covers the child's clothing is preferable. Being clothed completely in white more powerfully symbolizes the child's being cleansed from sin and reborn in Baptism.

9. Should parishes provide baptismal candles?

Parishes typically provide baptismal candles. If, for some extraordinary reason, a parish does not, someone from the parish should be able to guide families in selecting a candle.

10. What is the role of a godparent after the child is baptized?

A godparent (or sponsor) "helps the baptized person to lead a Christian life in keeping with baptism and to fulfill faithfully the obligations inherent in

---

12. CCL, 855.
13. OBC, 63, 99, 126, 152, 288, 325.

it."[14] There are many ways in which godparents can do this, but above all, godparents should be living examples of faith for their godchildren. Attending Mass together, giving religious gifts, serving others in Christian charity as their godchildren grow older, and participating at liturgies when their godchildren celebrate the other sacraments are all ways that godparents can fulfill their role after the Baptism.

11. What are the requirements to be a godparent?

The requirements for being a godparent, or as noted in the *Code of Canon Law*, a "sponsor," are spelled out clearly in canons 872–874. Generally, godparents must be at least sixteen years old and designated by the parents of the child. They must be fully initiated Catholics, having received Baptism, Confirmation, and Eucharist. Godparents may not be a parent of the child who is being baptized. There may be one male godparent, one female godparent, or one of each.

Additionally, godparents must not have incurred any kind of canonical penalty, and they must be leading "a life of faith in keeping with the function to be taken on."[15] Potential godparents have most likely not received a formal canonical penalty (censure or excommunication for apostasy, heresy, or another extraordinarily grave sin). However, the "life of faith" stipulation is more ambiguous. That requirement may be problematic for baptized Catholics who are not actively practicing faith, or whose lifestyle or actions are not aligned with Catholic moral teaching.

A baptized non-Catholic is permitted to participate in the Baptism as a "witness,"[16] but that person cannot be formally recognized as a godparent; however, there is one exception. Because of "the close communion" between Catholics and Eastern Orthodox Christians, "for a just cause" an Eastern Orthodox person may serve as godparent "together with a Catholic godparent, at the baptism of a Catholic infant or adult, so long as there is provision for the Catholic education of the person being baptized, and it is clear that the godparent is a suitable one."[17]

---

14. CCL, 872.
15. CCL, 874 §1, 3°.
16. CCL, 874 §2.
17. *Directory for the Application of the Principles and Norms on Ecumenism* (DAPNE), 98B.

12. May a Catholic be a godparent at a non-Catholic Baptism?

At nearly all non-Catholic Baptisms, a Catholic may serve as a witness, but not as a godparent or sponsor. The lone exception is Baptism in an Eastern Orthodox Church. As per the *Directory for the Application of the Principles and Norms of Ecumenism*, Catholics are permitted to be godparents.

A Catholic is not forbidden to stand as godparent in an Eastern Orthodox church if he/she is so invited. In this case, the duty of providing for the Christian education binds in the first place the godparent who belongs to the church in which the child is baptized.[18]

> It is the Catholic understanding that godparents, in a liturgical and canonical sense, should themselves be members of the church or ecclesial community in which the baptism is being celebrated.
>
> —*Directory for the Application of Principles and Norms on Ecumenism*, 98

13. It can be an awkward or difficult situation if the Church does not accept the godparents the parents have chosen. How should parish staffs pastorally approach this situation?

Difficult situations arise when one or both of the proposed godparents do not meet all of the Church requirements. If a proposed godparent is baptized but not Catholic, the solution may be simply to ask that person to be a Christian witness. However, some situations are not so easily resolved—particularly if proposed godparents are Catholics who may be unsuitable because they are not living a "life of faith."[19] No matter how charitable and kind the explanation, informing parents that they will need to choose different godparents can lead to many hard feelings. Many people simply do not know that specific requirements exist before someone is chosen, and then it is too late.

To reduce this difficulty, parents should be informed at the earliest possible time that there are requirements to be a godparent of a Catholic child. These requirements, along with any additional diocesan or parish guidelines, should be posted and readily available on parish websites. If bulletins include

---

18. DAPNE, 98B.
19. CCL, 874 §1, 3°.

baptismal scheduling information, a brief statement about godparents can be included. When parents contact the church regarding Baptism, requirements for godparents should be shared immediately and at the same time as the baptismal preparation session information. Baptismal information—including requirements for godparents—can even be shared with couples as part of Marriage preparation.

However, no matter how much notice is given, there will still be instances when the chosen godparents are not accepted by Church requirements. Pastoral ministers should address these situations honestly and directly. In these cases, parents are often upset—not only because they have to find other godparents, but often because they have already asked someone to be a godparent and now they have to rescind the invitation. Both of these concerns need to be addressed. Ask parents about how they understand the role of godparent and the reasons why they chose particular individuals. Explain the Church's theology of the role of godparent—that it is not simply an honorary title but an important spiritual responsibility—and how the requirements are intended to ensure that godparents are ready to carry out that responsibility. There is no easy way to resolve these cases, but speaking candidly, compassionately, and with a genuine desire to accompany the parents through the process is the most loving response to a difficult pastoral situation.

14. May a priest or a deacon serve as a godparent and also preside at the Baptism?

The *Code of Canon Law* does not prohibit a priest or a deacon from serving as a godparent. In such cases, it is preferable that the priest or deacon not preside at the Baptism so that he can serve completely in his role as a godparent. If that priest or deacon does preside at the Baptism, he should fulfill that particular liturgical role and leave the designated "godparent" responses and actions to a second godparent. It should be clear that he is baptizing in his role as a priest or deacon—not as a godparent.

15. How do we help parents understand the nature of sin and Original Sin, especially in a culture that has difficulty with the concept of evil and Satan?

For many centuries, the Church's theological understanding of Baptism centered on the washing and cleaning of the baptized from Original Sin.

Helping parents understand this concept is indeed challenging. It is important to emphasize that while babies have not committed actual, personal sins, they are human beings. Like all human beings, they are imperfect and in need of salvation; they are "subject to ignorance, suffering, and the domination of death; and inclined to sin"[20] throughout their lives. This state of imperfection and tendency to sin are the results of Original Sin—something that no person, not even an infant, can escape.

To help parents understand Original Sin and its concrete consequences more deeply, one of the prayers of exorcism or the Renunciation of Sin and Satan may be used as part of baptismal preparation discussions. Ask parents what is the "lure of evil"[21] they fear for their children or what concerns them about the world with its temptations. Such a discussion helps to make clear that even though infants have not committed sins, they will be tempted to sin just as all people are throughout the course of their lives.

16. What happens to a child who dies without being baptized?

For many centuries, Catholic theologians spoke of limbo to refer to the eternal destiny of unbaptized children. Neither heaven nor hell, limbo was understood as proper for unbaptized children because they were subject to Original Sin and had not committed any personal sin worthy of punishment.[22] In 2007, the International Theological Commission of the Congregation of the Doctrine of the Faith released the document, *The Hope of Salvation for Infants Who Die without Being Baptized*. This document recognizes that limbo is a "possible theological opinion,"[23] but echoing the *Catechism of the Catholic Church*[24] and the *Order of Christian Funerals*,[25] the document emphasizes that the Church "expresses hope in the mercy of God, to whose loving care the [unbaptized] infant is entrusted."[26]

> As regards *children who have died without Baptism*, the Church can only entrust them to the mercy of God.
> —*Catechism of the Catholic Church*, 1261

---

20. CCC, 418.
21. OBC, 57, 94, 121, 145, 282, and 320.
22. See also pages 4 and 15.
23. *The Hope of Salvation for Infants Who Die without Being Baptized*, 41.
24. See CCC, 1261.
25. See the *Order of Christian Funerals* (OCF), part II (funeral rites for children).
26. *The Hope of Salvation for Infants Who Die without Being Baptized*, 100; see also page 15.

In accordance with this teaching, Catholic funeral rites "may be celebrated for children whose parents intended them to be baptized but who died before baptism."[27] In that case, the rites omit the baptismal symbols of sprinkling with holy water and the placing of the pall. Also, specific prayers for unbaptized children are used throughout the rites.

17. How are the rites celebrated when infants are baptized at the Easter Vigil?

The introduction to the *Order of Baptism of Children* explains how to arrange the ritual in order to maintain the integrity of the Vigil.[28] First, the rite of receiving the child is celebrated prior to the start of the Vigil.[29] The period of time immediately prior to the Vigil is often busy with final preparations, so this rite may be celebrated earlier in the day, as the Preparation Rites for the elect often are on Holy Saturday morning. Since the Rite of Reception takes place at a time before the Vigil, it may be done within the context of a Liturgy of the Word. However, "if appropriate," this may be omitted, "and the anointing with the Oil of Catechumens takes place."[30] Second, the celebration of Baptism, with the anointing with chrism and clothing in the white garment, takes place immediately after the blessing of the water as the Missal indicates. Third, the assent of the celebrant and community to the Profession of Faith is omitted, as are the presentation of lighted candle and the *Ephphatha* Rite. Finally, the conclusion of the rite is omitted.[31]

This being said, preparing the Order of Baptism to be celebrated during the Easter Vigil can be confusing—especially when others are receiving the sacraments of initiation (adults are being baptized and confirmed, adults are being received into full communion, children of catechetical age are being baptized and confirmed). In these cases, the rites in the third

> To illustrate the paschal character of Baptism, it is recommended that the Sacrament be celebrated at the Easter Vigil or on a Sunday, when the Church commemorates the Resurrection of the Lord.
>
> —*Order of Baptism of Children*, 9

---

27. OCF, 237.
28. See OBC, 28 §1–4.
29. See OBC, 28 §1.
30. OBC, 28 §1.
31. See OBC, 28 §1.

edition of *The Roman Missal* and the *Rite of Christian Initiation of Adults* should be used as the primary outlines, and the local diocesan Office of Worship can provide additional assistance.

18. If Baptism takes place at the Easter Vigil, how is the Rite of Receiving the Child celebrated?

As noted in question 17, when the Baptism of infants takes place at the Easter Vigil, the "rite of receiving the children is carried out . . . at a convenient time and place"[32] before the Vigil. It is not an option to omit the Rite of Receiving the Child, as it is an important moment of welcome for the family whose child is being baptized. The rite is to be celebrated in advance of the Vigil, but it seems especially well-suited for early in the day on Holy Saturday. Ideally, it is celebrated fully, complete with a simple a cappella song or hymn at the beginning, with readings from Scripture, the offering of intercessions, and even a procession into the church. Although the Liturgy of the Word may be omitted "if appropriate,"[33] this option should be used cautiously. The Prayer of Exorcism is said, and the anointing with the oil of catechumens also occurs.[34]

Because Holy Saturday is also the day in which adults are making their final preparations to be baptized this same evening, it seems worthwhile to combine the Rite of Receiving the Child with the Preparation Rites of the *Rite of Christian Initiation of Adults*.[35] If the rites are combined, follow the model given in RCIA, 187–192. Begin with a song, greet the child and family at the door, process into the church, read from Scripture, give a short homily, and then include the rites specific to the RCIA (Presentation of the Lord's Prayer, Recitation of the Creed, *Ephphatha* Rite, or the choosing of a baptismal name) and the child (the Prayer of Exorcism and the anointing with the oil of catechumens[36]). The conclusion and dismissal follow.

---

32. OBC, 28 §1.
33. OBC, 28 §1.
34. See OBC, 28 §1.
35. The Preparation Rites are optional rites celebrated on Holy Saturday morning with the elect, adults who are making final preparations to be baptized at the Easter Vigil. The Preparation Rites ready the elect to profess their faith and hear the Word of God. At these rites, the elect may be presented the Lord's Prayer, recite or "return" the Creed, participate in the *Ephphatha* Rite, or choose a baptismal name.
36. Regarding the Baptism of adults, parish teams should be aware that the United States bishops approved the omission of anointing adults preparing for Baptism with the oil of catechumens both in the celebration of Baptism and in the optional Preparation Rites on Holy Saturday. The anointing with the oil of catechumens is therefore reserved for use in the Period of the Catechumenate and the Period of Purification of Enlightenment. Adults are not anointed on Holy Saturday morning (see RCIA, 33 §7).

19. If a Baptism takes place during Easter Time, is the water reblessed?

During the Easter Vigil the waters of the font are blessed. This water should be used for all Baptisms taking place within Easter Time. The *Order of Baptism of Children* provides an alternate text to use if the water has been blessed. Although a "blessing and invocation of God over the water" is included, this short prayer does not rebless the water but rather acknowledges that God has called his children to this water "in the faith of the Church, / that they may have eternal life." The prayer asks that the "blessed water lead" the children "to spiritual rebirth."[37]

20. Is the *Order of Baptism of Children* to be used for baptizing infants or older children?

The introduction to the *Order of Baptism of Children* defines "children" or "infants" as "those who, since they have not yet reached the age of discretion, cannot profess the faith for themselves."[38] According to the *Code of Canon Law*, the "age of discernment" is understood as about seven years old.[39] Therefore, the *Order of Baptism of Children* is intended to be used for the Baptism of a child who is under seven years of age. The *Rite of Christian Initiation of Adults* should be used to initiate children who have reached the age of discernment.

21. Why does the Order of Baptism occur at different places in the church (door, body of church, font)? Why is this important or symbolic?

As discussed earlier, the processional and stational nature of the baptismal rites has great symbolic importance. First, it embodies that Christians are a pilgrim people, moving together toward God. Second, it enables the primary symbols to speak: the door of the church is where we are welcomed from the world into the house of God; the ambo is where the Word of God is proclaimed; the font is where we are washed and reborn and welcomed as Christians; the altar is from where we are strengthened, nourished, and sent forth to do God's work in the world. Moving from place to place emphasizes the unique symbolic importance of each of these elements.

---

37. OBC, 119.
38. OBC, 1.
39. See CCL, 97 §2.

22. May the Litany of Saints be omitted during the Order of Baptism?

In normal circumstances, that is, during the Order of Baptism for Several Children[40] and the Order of Baptism for One Child (within or without Mass), the Litany of Saints is to be prayed; there is no option to omit this text.[41] The litany is also to be prayed if Baptism is administered by a catechist[42] and during the Order of Bringing a Baptized Child to the Church.[43] However, the litany may be omitted if there is a large number of children to be baptized. The decision to omit the litany in this circumstance should be based upon the needs of the gathered assembly.[44] The *Order of Baptism of Children* provides no option for the litany to be sung or said if the child is in danger of death and a priest or deacon is not available. The Litany of Saints is only omitted at the Easter Vigil if no one is to be baptized.

23. Can the renewal of baptismal promises with the sprinkling rite take place during the Order of Baptism as at the Easter Vigil?

The renewal of baptismal promises with its accompanying sprinkling rite is not called for in the *Order of Baptism of Children*. This ritual should only take place during the Easter Vigil or Easter Sunday Masses. This is significant because the purpose of Lent and its traditional disciplines (prayer, fasting, and almsgiving) is to prepare the baptized for renewing their baptismal promises at Easter. To include the renewal of baptismal promises at another time minimizes the importance of Lent as preparation to celebrate Easter. Although the sprinkling rite without the renewal of baptismal promises may take place on any Sunday of the year, this does not happen when a Baptism takes place at Mass. When Baptisms occur during Sunday Mass, the opening rites are altered and the Penitential Act is omitted. Because the sprinkling rite may occur in place of the Penitential Act at Masses and this latter rite is omitted, there is no sprinkling rite.

---

40. See OBC, 48, 85, 272, and 310.
41. It should be noted that the Litany of Saints is referred to as the Invocation of the Saints in the revised rite; however, it still remains the traditional Litany.
42. See OBC, 140.
43. See OBC, 176.
44. See OBC, 114.

24. Is the Gloria always sung during the Order of Baptism?

The Gloria is always sung during ritual Masses (Baptism, Confirmation, weddings), including those weekday Masses occurring in Advent or Lent. If a Baptism occurs during Sunday Mass in Advent or Lent, the Gloria is to be omitted.[45] The Gloria is not sung if Baptism is celebrated without Mass.

25. Should an infant be immersed? Should the water be poured?

Water must directly touch the skin of the child for a valid Baptism—both immersion and pouring (infusion) are permitted forms of Baptism. The rite lists immersion as the first of the two options, so as long as the font is suitable, immersion most richly symbolizes the child's complete dying and rising with Christ in the baptismal water of the font. The Byzantine, Ukrainian, and other Eastern Catholic Churches have long maintained this tradition through the "triple immersion": lowering infants entirely into the font three times, once for each person of the Trinity. Even when water is poured, the infant should still be lowered (or an older child should put his head down) as far as possible into the font.[46]

> Baptism is to be conferred either by immersion or pouring; the prescripts of the conference of bishops are to be observed.
>
> —*Code of Canon Law*, 854

26. What is the oil that is used during the celebration?

In the Orders of Baptism for Several Children and One Child (within and without Mass), two separate oils are used. The first is the oil of catechumens, which is used to anoint the child's breast immediately after the Prayer Of Exorcism so that Christ may "protect" the child with his "strength."[47] The second is the sacred chrism, which marks the child as a member of Christ's Body who is "Priest, Prophet and King."[48] The oil of catechumens is blessed

---

45. See GIRM, 53.
46. Even if parents intellectually understand the rich symbolism of this rite, some parents are hesitant to have their infants baptized by immersion even if that is the practice of the parish. Ways to address those concerns are discussed on page 63.
47. OBC, 50, 87, 275, and 313.
48. OBC, 62, 98, 125, 151, 178, 287, and 324.

and the sacred chrism is consecrated by the bishop of the diocese during the annual Chrism Mass. They usually consist of blessed olive oil, and an additional balsam fragrance is added to the chrism. Chrism is also used for anointing in Confirmation, the ordination of priests and deacons, and the dedication of a new altar and church. In the Order of Baptism for a Large Number of Children, the first anointing is omitted.

27. Why can't the Trinitarian formula be changed to Creator, Redeemer, and Sanctifier? Why don't we baptize only "in Christ" or "in God"?

First, there is no option to change the texts of the baptismal liturgy. If the option were provided, the rubrics would advise that "these or similar words" could be used. Recall that the *Constitution on the Sacred Liturgy* stresses that no one, "not even if he is a priest, may on his own add, remove, or change anything in the liturgy."[49]

> **N.**, I BAPTIZE YOU IN THE NAME OF THE FATHER,
> AND OF THE SON,
> AND OF THE HOLY SPIRIT.
>
> —*Order of Baptism of Children*, 60

There is also a significant theological reason for not altering the words of the Trinitarian language. The Trinitarian language of the baptismal formula is strongly rooted in both Scripture and Tradition. It is used not only by Catholics, but by many other Christian denominations. The Trinity consists of three persons in relationship with each other, yet they are also one God. Baptizing in the name of the Father, of the Son, and of the Holy Spirit affirms both the fullness of each person of the Trinity and the profound relationship between them—a relationship that we ourselves enter into through Baptism.

Using alternate names such as "Creator, Redeemer, and Sanctifier" reduces the persons of the Trinity to their function, thereby distorting the fullness of each person and their relationship to each other. Such distortion is a heresy known as modalism. For that reason, any Baptism using alternate terms—as well as any Baptism that omits one or more persons of the Trinity—is invalid.[50] In such cases, the child would need to be rebaptized.

---

49. CSL, 22 §3.
50. For more on the prohibition against alternate baptismal formulas, see "A New Response of the Congregation for the Doctrine of the Faith on the Validity of Baptism" by Msgr. Antonio

28. How can we incorporate liturgical formation in baptismal preparation for parents? How do we help parents to understand the symbolic significance of the rituals?

One simple way is to use elements of the rite as the basis for prayer at the start of each baptismal preparation session. Rather than simply saying the Lord's Prayer or an improvised prayer, read one of the Scripture passages provided in the rite. Light a candle and ask parents to bring their own baptismal candles (if they can find them!). Prepare a bowl of holy water so that everyone can bless themselves. The prayer need not be long, but it should reflect baptismal symbolism and themes.

There are many other ways to incorporate liturgical formation. While reading and discussing the rite can be helpful, as can watching videos of Baptisms taking place, actually experiencing a Baptism is the best way to be formed liturgically. Invite parents-to-be to attend a Baptism; talk with them afterward about what they noticed and what questions they have. This reflection on the experience of the sacramental rite is called mystagogy. *Mystagogy* means to "break open the mystery." It is a lifelong process that calls each baptized person to daily reflect upon their experience of Christ in our sacramental life. The "mystery" in mystagogy is the life, death, and Resurrection of Christ. We are called to contemplate our encounter with the Paschal Mystery and name how we are being transformed by God's saving love. There is no substitute for sacramental catechesis that springs directly from experiencing a celebration of that sacrament. The symbols and rituals of Baptism—the tracing of the cross, the water, the oils—come alive when they are experienced firsthand.

29. How do we prepare baptismal celebrations (during or without Mass) that connect the whole parish?

Often, parishioners feel disconnected from Baptism because it is celebrated without Mass. Even when Baptism is celebrated during Mass, parishioners feel disconnected when they cannot see, cannot hear, and cannot participate

---

Miralles, www.vatican.va/roman_curia/congregations/cfaith/documents/rc_con_cfaith_doc_20080201_validity-baptism-miralles_en.html.

meaningfully by singing, speaking the responses, following along with a worship aid, or even seeing what is happening. Careful and intentional celebration of the Order of Baptism is crucial. Invite parishioners to attend Baptisms celebrated without Mass. Schedule parish ministers to serve at these liturgies: servers, music ministers (especially teens), readers, and hospitality members. Visually ensure that all can see the primary symbols of the font and the water. Choose singable acclamations, responses, and songs or hymns and provide a worship aid so that everyone can follow the rite. The best way to help parishioners feel connected to these sacramental rites is to encourage their participation:

> I invite all Christians, everywhere, at this very moment, to a renewed personal encounter with Jesus Christ, or at least an openness to letting him encounter them.
> —*Evangelii gaudium*, 3

> The main way that parishioners participate in Christian initiation is by their presence and participation. The joyful participation of the faithful in the rites of the catechumenal process is felt and appreciated.[51]

After Baptism is celebrated, continue to bring the newly baptized and the parish community together. Celebrate Paschal Vespers during Easter Time, host catechetical gatherings with baptismal activities, invite families to baptismal anniversary parties and send baptismal anniversary cards—all of these activities and mementos help parents to understand concretely that their children have been baptized into a relationship with God and the Church community.[52]

30. What blessings may be celebrated before and after the Baptism of a child?

The *Book of Blessings* includes six blessings in chapter I, providing opportunities for the parish to be present with the family during baptismal preparation and following a Baptism:[53]

---

51. Rita Burns Senseman, Victoria M. Tufano, Paul Turner, D. Todd Williamson. *Guide for Celebrating® Christian Initiation with Children* (Chicago: Liturgy Training Publications, 2017), p. 128. Although these comments refer to children participating in the RCIA process, they also apply to infant Baptism.
52. Specific pastoral suggestions appear throughout this book, especially in the "Evangelization" (p. 125) and "Preparation Team" (p. 20) sections.
53. Chapter I of the *Book of Blessings* includes numerous other blessings related to marriage and family (for example, sons and daughters, parents after miscarriage).

- Order for the Blessing of Parents before Childbirth: This blessing may be celebrated "at any time during the pregnancy."[54] It helps to evangelize new parents and affirms that the Church is already praying for the family and seeks to deepen the parents' relationship with the Church before the birth of their child.

- Order for the Blessing of a Mother before Childbirth: This blessing is similar to the Order for the Blessing of Parents before Childbirth, however, it is to be used "when only the mother is present."[55] Its readings and prayers focus on Mary and her example of motherhood.

- Order for the Blessing of a Child Not Yet Baptized: This blessing is especially suitable if there is a significant delay between birth and Baptism. It is "similar to the blessings imparted during the catechumenate," and it includes the tracing of the Sign of the Cross on the children as a sign that they are "being prepared for the reception of baptism."[56]

- Order for the Blessing of Baptized Children: This blessing may be used on any number of occasions, but it is especially well suited for celebrating the anniversary of a child's Baptism.

- Order for the Blessing of a Mother after Childbirth: This blessing should be used "only for a mother who was unable to take part in the celebration of her child's baptism."[57]

- Order for the Blessing of Parents and an Adopted Child: This blessing celebrates the welcoming of an adopted child into a family and may be celebrated whether the child is baptized or not. It powerfully evangelizes by ritually affirming the adoption of the child and expressing the Church's love and support for the family.

The United States Conference of Catholic Bishops provides an additional blessing not found in the *Book of Blessings,* the *Rite for the Blessing of a Child in the Womb.* This blessing, approved for use in English and Spanish in 2012, recognizes "that all life is a gift from God," and it is "with joy and compassion" that "the Church welcomes . . . mothers . . . [coming] to the

---

54. BB, 216.
55. BB, 215.
56. BB, 156.
57. BB, 237. The *Book of Blessings* also provides a blessing for parents who suffered a miscarriage; see chapter I, 279–301.

Church seeking a blessing for their unborn child."[58] This blessing may take place within or without Mass; separate rites are provided for each option.

31. How are the blessings for parents celebrated?

The structure of the orders of blessing reflects the Church's belief that blessings are "signs that have God's word as their basis and that are celebrated from motives of faith."[59] Every blessing, then, has essential components: "the proclamation of the word of God" and "the praise of God's goodness and the petition for his help."[60] With the exception of the Order for the Blessing of Parents and an Adopted Child and the *Rite for the Blessing of a Child in the Womb*, the aforementioned blessings include two forms: a longer rite and a shorter rite. While specific elements will vary among the individual blessings, they all have the same general structure: a longer rite with an Introductory Rite (with Sign of the Cross, greeting, and brief explanation of the blessing), reading from Scripture, intercessions with the Lord's Prayer, blessing, and Concluding Rite. A shorter rite includes a simple greeting, short reading from Scripture, and the prayer of blessing. The decision to use the longer or shorter rite is left to the discretion of the presiding minister based on the pastoral circumstances (that is, the presence or absence of musicians and other ministers, the time and location of the blessing).

Consequently, the ideal time to celebrate these blessings is whenever a group of the faithful has gathered, such as immediately after Mass or immediately before or after a parish celebration of the Liturgy of the Hours. They may also be celebrated during catechetical events, baptismal preparation sessions, or even parish social gatherings, especially those welcoming new parishioners. Consider blessing parents periodically throughout the year. This could be combined with baptismal formation sessions beginning with prayer and including social time. Invite parents, members of the baptismal preparation formation team, and other ministries of the parish to gather in the church or parish chapel. Parents can be encouraged to invite the godparents as well as other family members. If they have other children they can bring them as well. This should be a family event—domestic and parish!

While these blessings may take place anywhere, celebrating these rites at an appropriate location in or around the church or a chapel is ideal. There

---

58. *Rite for the Blessing of a Child in the Womb*, 1.
59. BB, 10.
60. BB, 20.

are many options for preparing the liturgical environment, both indoors and even outdoors. Blessings for expectant parents or mothers could take place near a statue or image of the Holy Family, of Mary (or Mary and Jesus), or even near a Nativity scene. The Blessing of a Mother after Childbirth could take place near the baptistery or font. If a blessing takes place celebrated in a home or a classroom, it is best celebrated in or facing an area conducive to prayer, particularly if a crucifix, Bible, or other religious images are present.

Since the orders of blessing follow the same general pattern, the following pastoral suggestions pertaining to the Order of Blessing Parents before Childbirth can be used as guidance for preparing a liturgical celebration of the Word for the other longer forms of the blessings taking place without Mass. The suggestions that follow presume that the blessing is being led by an ordained minister in a church or chapel.[61] Although this blessing may be presided over by a priest, deacon, or layperson, it is appropriate for the pastor to preside so that he can get to know the parents and be present to them in a deeper way. Lit candles and flowers may be placed around a statue or icon of the Holy Family. Worship aids with the hymns, responses, and other musical texts should be given by hospitality ministers (members of the baptismal preparation team).

Although an entrance procession is not mentioned in the order of blessing, as a celebration of the Word and a liturgical rite of the Church, it is appropriate for a procession to be included. The procession does not need to be elaborate—cross-bearer followed by the priest celebrant is sufficient. The server should be vested in an alb or cassock and the priest may be vested in an alb and stole. The gathering song accompanies the procession and provides the assembly a chance to gather. Consider singing hymns such as "God beyond All Names," "Servant Song" by Richard Gillard, "O God, You Search Me" by Bernadette Farrell, "Like a Weaned Child" by Bob Hurd, "Wonder of Wonders," "O God beyond All Praising," or settings of the Magnificat (if this isn't chosen in place of the Responsorial Psalm). For this type of liturgy, the opening song does not need to be boisterous; a more gentle hymn is appropriate.

---

61. If a lay person presides, the blessing may look quite different. Besides the texts and gestures specific to the lay presider, there may be no procession, no vestments (although the minister may be vested in an alb), there may be less music or unaccompanied music, and it may not occur in a chapel (perhaps it occurs in a formation or catechetical room). If the blessing does not occur in a chapel, there will be no ambo, and the readings may be proclaimed from a binder or a Bible or a single copy of the *Book of Blessings* may be shared from among the group.

After the entrance song, the priest greets the assembly and "prepares those present for the blessing."[62] The *Book of Blessings* provides the text for him to say. For this particular blessing, the text recognizes that God is the source of creation and a child is the fruit of Marriage. It looks forward to the Sacrament of Baptism in which the child "will receive the gift of divine life itself."

After the priest prepares the assembly for the blessing, he may invite those who have gathered to be seated for the proclamation of the Word. There is no opening prayer—the readings begin immediately. The order of blessing recommends the account of the birth of Samuel. The full text of the reading is found in the *Book of Blessings*, and this ritual book can be used for the proclamation of the reading. Parishes should consider investing in multiple copies of the book so that both the priest and the reader can use their own copies. Just as at other liturgical rites, the reading should be proclaimed from the ambo. One of the baptismal preparation team members may be invited to proclaim the reading.

The *Book of Blessings* also provides two options from the Gospel according to Luke. Although these two readings are perfectly acceptable, keep in mind there is no Gospel acclamation, and reading a Gospel account in this context without the acclamation can be awkward and confusing to those in attendance. Should they stand? Should they say "Glory to you, O Lord"? Should they sign their forehead, lips, and mouth? It seems better pastoral practice to select a reading from the Old or New Testament instead of from the Gospel, especially since a Responsorial Psalm may follow the text.

Psalm 33 is the suggested text for the Responsorial Psalm. A cantor and accompanist may be invited to assist with the music so that the psalm is sung. Use a musical setting that is already familiar to the parish community. The order of blessing does provide the option to sing another suitable song. The Canticle of Mary is an acceptable substitute. Consider responsorial settings that are familiar to your parish, for example, "Holy Is Your Name" by David Haas.

The priest may decide to provide a brief explanation of the biblical text. This is a wonderful opportunity to speak about the fruits of marriage in the gift of children, the duty of parents to raise their children in the Catholic faith, and the role of the parish community in modeling Christian discipleship.

It is good to keep in mind the beauty of silence. Consider adding moments of silence to follow the reading from Samuel, the Responsorial Psalm, and the explanation of the reading.

---

62. BB, 221.

After the explanation of the reading and the moment of silence, the priest stands and motions for the assembly to stand as well. The litany is then said. The text may be adapted as necessary; the text provided in the *Book of Blessings* praises God for giving parents Mary and Joseph as a model for "loving parents" and for blessing the Marriage act with the gift of children. The ritual text recommends the response, "Blessed are you, O Lord, for your loving kindness." Consider chanting the verses and the response. Musical settings of the Responsorial Psalms for Mass may be appropriately used and be similar in text to what is provided in the *Book of Blessings* such as the antiphon for Psalm 103 and Psalm 104 ("O bless the Lord, O bless the Lord, my soul") by John Schiavone (GIA) and Robert J. Batastini (GIA) or the antiphon for Psalm 111 ("I thank you, Lord, for your faithfulness and love") by Randolph Currie (GIA).

The litany concludes with the praying of the Lord's Prayer and then the blessing of parents. At this time, the expecting parents may be invited to come forward and stand before the priest. He extends both hands over the parents and says the prayer of blessing.[63] The three-fold final blessing and dismissal concludes the order of blessing if an ordained minister presides. A lay minister concludes "by singing himself or herself with the sign of the cross and saying"[64] a simple blessing that invokes the protection of Mary and Joseph upon the expectant parents.

After the dismissal the parents may go back to their seats in the pew while a closing song is sung. Since the order of blessing began with a liturgical procession, it makes sense to end with one. The server with the processional cross leads the simple procession followed by the presider. Consider singing a hymn of thanksgiving such as "For the Beauty of the Earth," "O God beyond All Praising," "Let All Things Now Living," or even a song in honor of the Blessed Virgin Mary's motherhood such as "Mother Maiden, Meek and Mild." Settings of the Magnificat are appropriate here as well.[65]

---

63. An ordained minister extends both hands over the parents while saying the prayer of blessing, whereas a lay ministers "says the prayer with hands joined" (BB, 228).

64. BB, 230.

65. Pastoral ministers should be aware that the *Book of Blessings* does not note proper posture. It would appropriate for the assembly to stand during the Introductory Rite, be seated for the Liturgy of the Word, stand for the Gospel, and remain standing for the rest of the rite.

RESOURCES

Church Documents and Ritual Books

- *Book of Blessings*. Among many other offerings, this book includes blessings for children (baptized and not yet baptized), parents before childbirth, and mothers before and after childbirth. It also includes two formularies for the blessing of a new baptistery or baptismal font: one for when Baptism is being celebrated, and one for when it is not. Many, though not all, of the blessings may be led by a layperson.
- *Built of Living Stones: Art, Architecture, and Worship*. Issued by the United States Conference of Catholic Bishops in 2000, these guidelines provide parishes with theological and liturgical guiance for building and renovating churches as well as for preparing the liturgical environment. The document includes pastoral commentary concerning the baptistry.
- *Catechism of the Catholic Church, Second Edition*. Baptism is referenced at points throughout the text, most fully in paragraphs 1212–1284.
- *Code of Canon Law*. Canons 849–878 address the juridical requirements for a valid and licit celebration of the Sacrament of Baptism, including its time, place, proper ministers, and guidelines for sponsors (godparents).
- *The Hope of Salvation for Infants Who Die without Being Baptized*. Issued by the International Theological Commission in October of 2004, this document explores the question of salvation for infants who died before being baptized.
- *Lectionary for Mass*. In addition to providing the Scripture readings for Mass, the Lectionary also includes the Scripture texts prescribed for use in the *Rite of Baptism for Children*.
- *Order of Baptism of Children* and *Rite of Christian Initiation for Adults*. Numerous editions are published in a variety of styles and bindings, some for liturgical use and others for personal study.

- *The Roman Missal.* The current edition includes two ritual Mass formularies (sets of Mass prayers, antiphons, etc.) for the conferral of Baptism. They can be found with the other ritual Masses in section I ("For the Conferral of the Sacraments of Christian Initiation"), number 3 ("For the Conferral of Baptism"), options A and B.
- *Sing to the Lord: Music in Divine Worship.* This comprehensive 2007 document from the United States Conference of Catholic Bishops addresses many aspects of liturgical music. Sections 207–212 directly address Baptism of children, both during and without Mass.

Theological and Historical Resources

- Johnson, Maxwell. *Images of Baptism: Number Six, Forum Essays.* Chicago: Liturgy Training Publications, 2001. This book explores four rich theological interpretations of Baptism: as participation in the death, burial, and Resurrection of Christ; as new birth and adoption by water and the Holy Spirit; as the sacrament and seal of the Holy Spirit; and as incorporation into the body of Christ.
- Johnson, Maxwell, ed. *Living Water, Sealing Spirit: Readings on Christian Initiation.* Collegeville, MN: Liturgical Press, 1995. Edited by Maxwell Johnson, this compilation of twenty essays considers the sacraments of initiation from a variety of theological and historical perspectives. The final three essays specifically address issues surrounding infant Baptism.
- Johnson, Maxwell, ed. *The Rites of Christian Initiation: Their Evolution and Interpretation.* Collegeville, MN: Liturgical Press, 2007. This authoritative, comprehensive book details the history of Baptism and initiation throughout the Christian world: East and West, Catholic and Protestant.
- Stice, Randy. *Understanding the Sacraments of Initiation: A Rite-Based Approach.* Chicago: Liturgy Training Publications, 2016. Guiding readers through the Rites of Baptism, Confirmation, and Eucharist, this book examines each of the rites' Old Testament foundations, liturgical history, and sacramental theology, exploring the way in which the sacraments of initiation affect and influence one's daily Christian life.
- Turner, Paul. *Ages of Initiation: The First Two Christian Millennia.* Collegeville, MN: Liturgical Press, 2000. This book/CD combination

provides an annotated timeline of the sacraments of initiation, including the practice of infant Baptism, throughout Church history. The printed book summarizes the practices and theological understandings of Baptism, Confirmation, and Eucharist, while the CD provides fuller explanations and quotations from primary sources.

- Witczak, Michael. *Lex Orandi: The Sacrament of Baptism*. Collegville, MN: Liturgical Press, 2011. This text offers a deep analysis of the current Roman Catholic baptismal rites. Focusing on symbolic meaning and language, it considers both infant Baptism and adult Baptism: the shape of the rituals, the words of their Scripture readings and prayers, and their theological meaning.

Pastoral Resources

For Pastoral Ministers

- Archdiocese of Chicago. *Infant Baptism: A Sourcebook for Parishes (Welcomed by Name)*. Chicago: Loyola Press, 2012. Developed by the Archdiocese of Chicago, this binder (teacher's edition) offers everything from catechetical materials to assessments for parish ministers who are involved in preparing and celebrating infant Baptism.

- Baker, Robert J., Larry J. Nyberg, and Victoria M. Tufano, eds. *A Baptism Sourcebook*. Chicago: Liturgy Training Publications, 1993. Taken from prose, poetry, hymnody, Scripture and liturgical and patristic texts, this anthology of texts unfolds the mystery of Baptism as an event that extends into every moment of life. Section titles suggest the richness of symbols and gestures of christening: election, faith and creed, water, naming, godparents, anointing, dressing, light, festivity, and mission.

- Gensler, Gail, Timothy Johnston, Corinna Laughlin, and Kyle Lechtenberg. *Disciples Making Disciples: Print and Digital Resources for Forming the Assembly*. Chicago: Liturgy Training Publications, 2017. This collection of bulletin inserts can be used to help form the assembly in their understanding of Christian initiation. Although this resource is primarily focused on the RCIA, it does provide inserts concerning the dignity of Baptism and the responsibility it endows upon the Christian faithful.

- Rojcewicz, Rebekah. *Baptism Is a Beginning / El Bautismo es un comienzo: Bilingual Reproducible Handouts for Infant Baptism Preparation*. Chicago:

Liturgy Training Publications, 2009. This book with CD-ROM provides parishes with all they need to prepare parents and families, godparents, and sponsors for the Baptism of a child and for continuing support and formation after the Baptism. Eighteen different pamphlets can be reproduced for distribution to families and are enriched by the insights of Sofia Cavalletti, founder of the Catechesis of the Good Shepherd.

- Senseman, Rita Burns, Victoria Tufano, Paul Turner, and D. Todd Williamson. *Guide for Celebrating Christian Initiation with Children*. Chicago: Liturgy Training Publications, 2017. As part of the *Preparing Parish Worship*™ series, this book combines a theological and historical overview of the Christian initiation of children of catechetical age with practical advice and a step-by-step guide to preparing vibrant and life-giving liturgies. The book walks through the rituals with children, noting best practice and options. The liturgical environment and liturgical music, as well as liturgical ministers and parish evangelization are addressed.

- Tufano, Victoria, ed. *Catechesis and Mystagogy: Infant Baptism*. Chicago: Liturgy Training Publications, 1996. Edited by Victoria Tufano, this book offers insights for catechists who are responsible for baptismal preparation and other ministers who prepare baptismal celebrations. It includes bulletin inserts that may be reproduced in order to deepen parishioners' understanding of Baptism and its role in the sacramental life of a parish.

For Parents, Godparents, and Families

- Bowman, Peg. *Welcomed by Name: Our Child's Baptism*. Chicago: Loyola Press, 2003. Available in two editions—one for parents, one for godparents—this booklet offers an overview to help them prepare for their roles in the celebration of Baptism.

- Gasslein, Bernadette. *Your Child's Baptism, Revised Edition*. Toronto: Novalis, 2015. Featuring full-color photos, this short book is particularly suited for parents who are relatively unfamiliar with Baptism, its elements, and their meaning. (Note: This book was published in Canada and is distributed in the United States through Liturgical Press.)

- Hamma, Robert M. *Together at Baptism*. Notre Dame, IN: Ave Maria Press, 2012. Written for parents, this book offers a detailed explanation of Baptism and its meaning. It focuses on the rite itself through a series of two-page spreads: rubrics on the left page, a short catechetical explanation and reflection question on the right page. It also includes Scripture readings, instructions for making a baptismal candle, and a "Family Renewal of Baptism" prayer service.

- *Kids and the Sacraments: Baptism.* Chicago: Loyola Press, 2015. Intended for young children, such as those whose infant siblings will soon be baptized, this DVD explains Baptism and its significance by incorporating interviews with children, explanations from a priest, and various other multimedia components. This video is also available to rent on Amazon.

- Ramshaw, Elaine. *The Godparent Book.* Chicago: Liturgy Training Publications, 2007. This book offers an abundance of ideas for things that godparents and godchildren can do from before Baptism through adulthood. Included are suggestions for building the relationship by sharing the memories, thoughts, values, prayers, and seasons of Christian life.

- Strand, Emily. *Your Baby's Baptism.* Liguori, MO: Liguori Publications, 2014. As part of the *Liguori Sacramental Preparation Series,* this baptismal preparation program includes a variety of materials: a guide for parents, a guide for catechetical leaders, and a "Welcome to God's Family" DVD. Elements of the program are also available in Spanish.

- Turner, Paul. *Your Child's Baptism.* Paul Turner. Chicago: Liturgy Training Publications, 1999. This small book clearly and concisely addresses many questions that parents have about Baptism: both the rite itself and specific concerns (that is, baptizing children of single parents or parents who were married outside the Church, selection of godparents, making a gift to the parish). A revised edition is scheduled to be published in early 2018.

Bulletin Inserts

LTP publishes a number of bulletin inserts about Baptism which may be downloaded for free in English and Spanish.

- *How Does Baptism Change Us*? by Kristopher W. Seaman: www.pastoralliturgy.org/resources/HowDoesBaptismChangeUs.pdf (English) and www.pastoralliturgy.org/resources/Comonoscambiaelbautismo.pdf (Spanish).

- *What Happened at My Baptism?* by Kristopher W. Seaman: www.pastoralliturgy.org/resources/WhatHappenedatMyBaptism.pdf (English) and www.pastoralliturgy.org/resources/Quesucedioenmibautismo.pdf (Spanish).

- *Baptismal Symbols at Funerals* by Kristopher W. Seaman: www.pastoralliturgy.org/resources/BaptismalsymbolsatFunerals.pdf (English) and www.pastoralliturgy.org/resources/Lossimbolosbautismalesenlasexequias.pdf (Spanish).

- *A Sign of Our Belonging* by Trish Sullivan Vanni: www.pastoralliturgy.org/resources/ASignofOurBelonging.pdf (English) and www.pastoralliturgy.org/resources/Unsignodenuestrapertenencia.pdf (Spanish).

- *The Holy Oils* by Kristopher W. Seaman: www.pastoralliturgy.org/resources/TheHolyOils.pdf (English) and www.pastoralliturgy.org/resources/LosSantosOleos.pdf (Spanish).

- *Why Are Babies Baptized during Mass?* by Kristopher W. Seaman: www.pastoralliturgy.org/resources/0905ReproRsrc.pdf.

- *Celebrating Sacraments during Easter* by Darren M. Henson, STL: www.pastoralliturgy.org/resources/0703ReproRsrc.pdf.

- *The Mission of the Baptized* by Maureen A. Kelly, MA: www.pastoralliturgy.org/resources/0603ReproRsrc.pdf.

GLOSSARY

Acclamation: A brief, joyful liturgical response, such as "Alleluia," "Amen," or "Blessed be God!"

Adult: For the purpose of sacramental initiation, a person who has reached the age of reason (also called the age of discretion or catechetical age), usually regarded to be seven years of age, is an adult. A person who has reached that age is to be initiated into the Church according to the *Rite of Christian Initiation of Adults* and receive the three sacraments of initiation together; however, the catechesis should be adapted to the individual's needs. Before this age, the person is considered an infant and is baptized using the *Order of Baptism of Children.*

Age of Reason: For the purpose of sacramental initiation, a person who reaches the age of reason (also called the age of discretion or catechetical age), usually regarded to be seven years of age, is an adult. A person who has reached that age is to be initiated into the Church according to the *Rite of Christian Initiation of Adults* and receive all three sacraments of initiation together; however, the catechesis should be adapted to their needs. Before this age, the person is considered an infant and is baptized using the *Order of Baptism of Children.*

Affusion: The method of administering Baptism by which the minister pours water over the head of the candidate while pronouncing the baptismal formula. Although affusion is probably the most common way of administering the sacrament in the Latin Church, Baptism by immersion (also called infusion) is preferred because of its fuller symbolism.

Ambo: The place from which all the Scripture readings are proclaimed and the homily may be preached during liturgy; a pulpit or lectern. The ambo is also used for the singing of the *Exsultet*, for announcing the intentions of the Universal Prayer, and for the leading of the Responsorial Psalm. The term is derived from a Greek word for "raised place."

Ambry: A place for the storing of the holy oils (chrism, oil of catechumens, and oil of the sick). In older churches the ambry was a niche in the wall, often with a locking door. In new and renovated churches, the ambry is often located near the baptismal font and constructed so that the vessels containing the holy oils can be seen.

Apostles' Creed: The ancient baptismal statement of the Church's faith. The questions used in the celebration of Baptism correspond to the statements of the Apostles' Creed.

Baptismal Font: The pool or basin at which the Sacrament of Baptism is administered.

Baptistery: A separate section of the church building or even a separate building where the baptismal font is located and where Baptisms are performed; also spelled *baptistry*.

Blessing: Any prayer that praises and thanks God. In particular, blessing describes those prayers in which God is praised because of some person or object, and thus the individual or object is seen to have become specially dedicated or sanctified because of the prayer of faith.

Book of Blessings: The ritual book that contains blessings for numerous occasions. Many of the blessings may be given during the celebration of Mass, and so most of the rites include forms both for within Mass and without Mass. In a number of cases, the rubrics specify that a lay minister may lead a particular ritual without Mass.

Catechesis: Instruction and spiritual formation in the faith, teachings, and traditions of the Church.

Celebrant: The ordained presiding minister at worship.

Child: For the purposes of Christian initiation, one who has not yet reached the age of discernment (age of reason, presumed to be about seven years of age) and therefore cannot profess personal faith. *See also* infant.

Chrism: One of the three holy oils. It is consecrated by the bishop at the Chrism Mass and used at the Baptism of infants, at Confirmation, at the ordination of priests and bishops, and at the dedication of churches and altars. Chrism is scented, usually with balsam, which creates a distinctive and pleasing aroma; it is the only one of the three sacramental oils that is scented. Chrism is stored in the ambry and in oil stocks that are often labeled SC for "sacred chrism."

Confirmation: The sacrament that continues the initiation process begun in Baptism and marks the sealing of the Holy Spirit. It is administered through an anointing with chrism on the forehead with the words, "N. be sealed with the Gift of the Holy Spirit," preceded by the imposition of hands.

Cope: A long, cape-like vestment. It may be worn in processions joined to a Mass (for example, the procession with palms on Palm Sunday) or at more solemn liturgical celebrations that occur without Mass (for instance, the Liturgy of the Hours or Benediction). The cope is normally worn only by an ordained minister.

Credence Table: The side table on which the vessels and articles needed for the celebration are placed when not in use, particularly during the celebration of the Eucharist.

Ephphatha: A rite of opening the ears and the mouth, associated with the celebration of Baptism. The rite, which has its origin in Mark 7:31–37, Jesus' healing of a deaf man, prays that the one being baptized may hear and profess the faith. It is an optional rite; it may be performed with adults as part of their preparation on Holy Saturday for initiation at the Easter Vigil or as part of the Order of Baptism, after the presentation of the lighted candle.

Evangelization: the continuing mission of the Church to spread the Gospel of Jesus Christ to all people.

Exorcism: A prayer or command given to cast out the presence of the devil. The *Order of Baptism of Children* includes a Prayer Of Exorcism, which takes place after the Litany of the Saints. The *Rite of Christian Initiation of Adults* includes prayers of exorcism as part of the rites belonging to the period of the catechumenate and as part of the scrutinies. There is a Rite of Exorcism for use in the case of possession; it may be used only with the express permission of a bishop and only by mandated priest-exorcists.

Explanatory Rites: Rites that take place immediately after a sacramental action that serve to amplify the meaning and effects of the sacrament. In the Baptism of children, for example, the anointing with chrism after Baptism, the clothing with a white garment, the giving of the lighted candle, and the *Ephphatha* prayer are all Explanatory Rites.

Font: Another name for the baptismal font.

Godparents: Members of the Christian community, chosen for their good example and their close relationship to the one being baptized, who are present at the celebration of Baptism and provide guidance and assistance to the one baptized afterward. In the case of adult Baptism, godparents assist with the final preparation and formation of the catechumens and at the Rite of Election testify to their readiness for initiation. In the Baptism of children, godparents assist the parents in raising the child in the faith and, at the celebration, profess the Church's faith with the parents. To be a godparent, a Catholic must have received all three sacraments of initiation and be living a life consistent with Catholic teaching. Only one godparent is required at Baptism, but if there are two, one is to be a male and one a female. A baptized non-Catholic may act as a Christian witness along with a Catholic godparent. In the *Code of Canon Law*, a godparent is referred to as a sponsor.[1]

Grace: The outpouring of God's love and help upon humanity which he gives freely and without merit.

Great Commission: The Risen Christ's instruction to his disciples to baptize others in the name of the Father, and of the Son, and of the Holy Spirit and to spread his Good News to all nations.[2]

Holy Oils: The collective name for the oil of catechumens, the oil of the sick and the sacred chrism, blessed and consecrated by the bishop on or near Holy Thursday and distributed to the parishes for use in the sacraments.

Holy Water: Water that has been blessed. Holy water is usually found in stoups, or fonts, at the entrances of churches so that individuals may bless themselves with it, reminding them of the waters of Baptism. It is also used when blessing objects and people. In many churches, a large, covered container of holy water is kept so that the faithful may take some home for devotional use.

Immersion: The method of administering Baptism in which the candidate is totally immersed three times in a font or pool. In the case of an older child or adult, and based on the construction of the font or pool, the minister may also stand in the pool. The baptismal formula is pronounced as the immersion takes place. Immersion is deemed the more suitable method for symbolizing participation in the death and Resurrection of Christ.[3]

---

1. See CCL, 872–874.
2. See Matthew 28:19.
3. See CI, 22.

Indelible: A permanent and spiritual mark imparted by participation in the sacraments.

Infant: *See* child.

Infusion: The method of administering Baptism by which the minister pours water over the head of the candidate while pronouncing the words, "**N.**, I baptize you in the name of the Father, and of the Son, and of the Holy Spirit."

Initiation: The process by which a person enters the faith life of the Church—Baptism, Confirmation, and Eucharist.

Lectionary for Mass: The book containing the Scripture readings proclaimed at Mass, including the Responsorial Psalms, for each day of the year. The Lectionary approved for use in the United States is published in several volumes. The Gospel readings are also contained in a separate *Book of the Gospels*.

Litany of the Saints: A litany that calls upon the saints to pray for the Church, believed to be the most ancient litany in the Church's worship. It is used in various forms during the Easter Vigil for the blessing of the baptismal font, during the Order of Baptism, during the dedication of a church, at ordinations, and as an option in the prayers for the commendation of the dying.

Oil of Catechumens: One of the three holy oils. It is used to anoint catechumens during their time of formation and infants in the Order of Baptism of Children. It is stored in a decanter or oil stock usually labeled OC.

Order: A prescribed form of a liturgical ritual, such as the *Order of Baptism of Children*, *Order of Christian Funerals*, or Order of Mass.

Order of Baptism of Children: The ritual book that gives the rites for the Baptism of children who have not yet attained the age of discretion (the age of reason), presumed to be about age seven.

Paschal Candle: The large candle that is inscribed, lighted, and carried in procession at the beginning of the Easter Vigil. During Easter Time it is given a prominent place near the ambo or in the middle of the sanctuary and is lit during Masses and other services throughout the fifty days of Easter Time. After Pentecost, it is kept in the baptistery and is lit during the celebration of Baptism. It is also lit at funerals, and may be placed at the head of the coffin. The Paschal candle must be a genuine candle made of wax, and renewed each year; there is to be only one Paschal candle in a church. It is also called the Easter candle.

Paschal Mystery: The saving mystery of Christ's passion, death, and Resurrection. It is the mystery that is celebrated and made present in every liturgy, and the mystery that every Christian is to imitate and be united with in everyday life. In general, then, it can also refer spiritually to any event in which the experience of joy arising through sorrow or new life coming out of death is achieved and experienced in union with Christ's own Death and Resurrection. While every liturgical celebration is founded on the Paschal Mystery, it is especially celebrated during the Paschal Triduum.

Pouring: The act of using a hand, a shell, or other vessel to place holy water onto the head of a person being baptized by infusion or affusion. Unlike sprinkling (when only a few drops of water touch the skin), pouring implies that a significant amount of water flows freely onto the person being baptized.

Rite: (1) The title of any official liturgical ceremony, such as the *Rite of Christian Initiation of Adults*. The term is sometimes interchangeable with the word *Order*, as in the Order of Mass or *Order of Christian Funerals*. The revised translations of ritual texts are using the word *Order* instead of *Rite*.

(2) A section of a larger ceremony, such as the Introductory Rites or the Concluding Rites of the Mass.

(3) A ritual family usually associated with a particular territory, which includes the individual traditions, feasts, canon law, ways of celebrating the sacraments, and approaches to theology. The two major rites in the Catholic Church are the Roman Rite and the Byzantine Rite (also used by Orthodox Christians).

Rite of Christian Initiation of Adults: The ritual book, part of the Roman Ritual, that gives the norms, directives, and ritual celebrations for initiating unbaptized adults and children who have reached catechetical age into Christ and incorporating them into the Church. The RCIA prescribes a sequence of periods and rites by which candidates transition from one stage to another, which culminate in the celebration of the sacraments of initiation, usually at the Easter Vigil.

The Roman Missal: The book or books containing the prayers, hymns, and Scripture readings prescribed for the celebration of Mass. Before the revision of the Missal in 1570, after the Council of Trent, the various texts were found in different books, but these were combined into one volume after the Council. The one volume Missal was commonplace until the Second Vatican Council. The present-day Missal, published in 1970 and currently in its third edition, is subdivided into several books: a book of prayers used by the priest, which is still called the "Missal" even though technically the book contains only part of the Missal; the Lectionary, which contains the Scripture readings; and the book of hymns and antiphons called the Gradual. Formularies for the Conferral of Baptism at Mass are found in the ritual Masses section of the Missal.

Sacraments of Christian Initiation: The Sacraments of Baptism, Confirmation, and Eucharist. All three sacraments are necessary to be fully initiated into the Church. Adults, including children of catechetical age, receive the three sacraments in one liturgy when being initiated into the Church.

Tracing of the Cross: Ritual action in which one person uses a finger (usually the right thumb) to trace a small cross on another person. During the Order of Baptism of Children, the presider, parents, and (optionally) godparents trace the cross on the forehead of the child who is to be baptized. The tracing of the cross also occurs in other Church rites, including the signing of the senses during the Rite of Acceptance into the Order of Catechumens.

White Garment: The clothing, often similar to an alb, which is given to someone immediately after Baptism. This garment is a sign that the newly baptized person has put on new life in Christ. It is used in the Baptism of both adults and children.

ACKNOWLEDGMENTS

Scripture readings are from the *New American Bible,* revised edition © 2010, 1991, 1986, 1970, Confraternity of Christian Doctrine, Washington, DC. Used with permission. All rights reserved. No part of the *New American Bible* may be reproduced without permission in writing from the copyright owner.

English translation of the *Catechism of the Catholic Church for the United States of America* © 1994, United States Catholic Conference, Inc.—Libreria Editrice Vaticana. English translation of the *Catechism of the Catholic Church Modifications from the Editio Typica* © 1997, United States Catholic Conference, Inc.—Libreria Editrice Vaticana. Used with permission.

Sing to the Lord: Music in Divine Worship © 2007 United States Conference of Catholic Bishops (USCCB), Washington, DC; *Built of Living Stones* © 2000, USCCB; National Statutes for the Catechumenate © 1986, USCCB; *Book of Blessings* © 1988, USCCB. Used by license of the copyright owner. All rights reserved.

Excerpts from *Documents on the Liturgy, 1963–1979: Conciliar, Papal, and Curial Texts* © 1982, International Commission on English in the Liturgy Corporation (ICEL); excerpts from the English translation of *Pastoral Care of the Sick: Rites of Anointing and Viaticum* © 1982, ICEL; excerpts from the English translation of *Rite of Christian Initiation of Adults* © 1985, ICEL; excerpts from the English translation of *The Roman Missal* © 2010, ICEL; excerpts from the English translation of *The Order of Baptism of Children* © 2017, ICEL. All rights reserved. Texts contained in this work derived whole or in part from liturgical texts copyrighted by the International Commission on English in the Liturgy (ICEL) have been published here with the confirmation of the Committee on Divine Worship, United States Conference of Catholic Bishops. No other texts in this work have been formally reviewed or approved by the United States Conference of Catholic Bishops.

Excerpts from *New Commentary on the Code of Canon Law,* by John P. Beal, James A. Coriden, and Thomas J. Green, Copyright © 2000 by The Canon Law Society of America. Paulist Press, Inc., New York/Mahwah, NJ. Reprinted by permission of Paulist Press, Inc. www.paulistpress.com.

The Glossary definitions were written by Dennis C. Smolarski, SJ, and Joseph DeGrocco © Liturgy Training Publications. "Ministerial Opportunities" on page 107 was written by Ann Dickinson Degenhard.

The baptismal candle on the cover and featured on pages 70, 122, 125, and 126 © Marklin Candle. Additional designs are found on their website: https://www.marklincandle.com/.